Thir

In a time of doctrinal _____ Christian
leaders, in particular, _____ them see and embrace
truth. Abendroth, Arc_____ _____wn have teamed together to provide
a richness of theological discussion with a depth of practical relevance
on a host of difficult areas within our common Christian conviction.
Everything around us urges compromise; these three authors urge
fidelity! Readers will find here a firmness that is not harsh combined
with a charity that is not compromise. May God be pleased to use this
excellent book to bring increased stability and growth to Christian
lives and churches.

Bruce A. Ware
Professor of Christian Theology
The Southern Baptist Theological Seminary, Louisville, KY

Things That Go Bump in the Church is a wonderfully readable, commu-
nicative, and comforting night-light for the inquiring Christian seeking guidance through the tough questions that are so often kept in the
shadows of the fellowship.

James White
Alpha and Omega Ministries

Imagine always eating chocolate cake and never partaking of vegetables. Have we simply become too addicted to the comfortable, too
addicted to being affirmed? Too soft? Even nature knows the dark night
of the soul precedes the light of dawn. Read this book and you'll see
how these hard doctrines, like our daily dose of broccoli, can be so
good for us.

Stephen J. Nichols
Research Professor of Christianity and Culture
Lancaster Bible College, PA

This book proves that sound teaching can be engagingly written and served with a dash of humor and punch. *Things That Go Bump in the Church* is hard-hitting yet pastoral in the best sense of that word. The authors are experienced pastors and students of God's Word and the history of theology. You will find yourself caught up with the flow of the text unawares as various controversial yet important doctrines are discussed. I recommend this book to Christians everywhere who desire to become mature disciples of Christ.

Jeffrey C. Waddington
Alliance of Confessing Evangelicals

Mike, Clint, and Byron have taken on some very important topics in this book for which I am grateful. For instance, the danger of mysticism is one of the most important topics, and it is biblically addressed in this book. The phony and dangerous spiritual warfare of "binding" demons and railing at demons is another lie that far too many self-professing Christians have believed, and this book ably refutes that lie with the power of God's Word. Finally, many Christians get providence and miracles confused and thus have bought the lie of signs and wonders via false teachers. Thank you Mike, Clint, and Byron for writing this book.

Brannon Howse
Host of Worldview Weekend Radio

THINGS THAT GO BUMP IN THE CHURCH

MIKE ABENDROTH
CLINT ARCHER
BYRON YAWN

HARVEST HOUSE PUBLISHERS
EUGENE, OREGON

Cover by Dugan Design Group, Bloomington, Minnesota

Cover photo © Stuart Monk / Fotolia

Mike Abendroth's author photo by Paige Crane Photography

This book is published in association with The Benchmark Group Agency, Nashville, TN (benchmark group1@aol.com)

THINGS THAT GO BUMP IN THE CHURCH

Copyright © 2014 by Mike Abendroth, Clint Archer, Byron Forrest Yawn
Published by Harvest House Publishers
Eugene, Oregon 97402
www.harvesthousepublishers.com

Library of Congress Cataloging-in-Publication Data
 Abendroth, Mike, 1960-
 Things that go bump in the church / Mike Abendroth, Clint Archer, Byron Forrest Yawn.
  pages cm
 ISBN 978-0-7369-5376-4 (pbk.)
 ISBN 978-0-7369-5377-1 (eBook)
 1. Theology, Doctrinal—Popular works. I. Title.
 BT77.A185 2014
 230—dc23
                                                                    2013023653

Printed in the United States of America

14 15 16 17 18 19 20 21 22 / BP-JH / 10 9 8 7 6 5 4 3 2 1

CONTENTS

PREFACE

One of my most treasured possessions is an old paperback Christian book. It is somewhat battered and dog-eared and the pages are yellowed at the edges. It also has one of those awful 1980s covers—a picture of a sunset—that were so popular among evangelicals back then. Aesthetically, it has all the appeal of a dated disco album. Yet that book is a treasure.

When I became interested in Christianity at the age of 17, I knew nothing about the faith. I had rarely been to church, except for the occasional carol service at Christmas. I had read very little of the Bible. I had no idea of what theology was. Yet as I left for university, the local Baptist pastor gave me this book—pretty battered, I seem to remember even by the time I received it—and my life changed forever. The book was *God's Words* and the author was J.I. Packer. It was not a book of striking originality, nor one of those for which Dr. Packer would be most famous; but it did something for me that transformed my thinking. It explained basic biblical concepts in language that even I, a neophyte believer, was able to grasp.

Basic books on solid issues are a vital part of the church's literature. It is one of the reasons catechisms were developed: to make sure that even the humblest believer with the least amount of spare time was able to learn the foundations and basic building blocks of the faith. In today's world, where fewer and fewer people even within Christian homes are brought up under solid preaching and taught basic catechetical theology, the need is even more urgent. That is why it is a pleasure to be able to write the preface for this volume. What the authors have done here is to provide a series of essays on matters of interest to the church, from the doctrine of hell to that of Christian freedom to the issue of proper local church eldership to homosexuality. The reader who takes the time to work through these essays will receive a good grounding in sound thinking about the Christian life, both doctrinally and practically.

Yet there is more to the Christian faith than simply providing contemporary explanations of Christian truth. An important element of this volume is the desire of the authors to be historically and ecclesiastically responsible. Thus, the text is replete with references to creeds and confessions, to the writings of respected men from the past, and to lessons that can be drawn from history. Readers will thus find themselves not simply connected to the Bible, but also to the church throughout the ages as it has sought to be faithful to her Lord.

Dr. Packer's book still sits on my bedside table. I confess that I consult it rarely these days. But it is there as a reminder that the basics are important and that those who teach us those basics, whether directly from the pulpit or in conversation over coffee or indirectly through books and other media, fulfill an important role in the lives of Christians. This book is of a similar caliber, and I trust that in years to come readers will remember the authors and the volume with the same affection and gratitude as I have for Dr. Packer and *God's Words*.

Carl R. Trueman
Westminster Theological Seminary, PA

FACING THE THINGS THAT
GO BUMP
IN THE CHURCH

You are soundly snoring in your bed. It's late, you're exhausted, and you're enjoying a blissful dreamscape powered by REM sleep. The next moment you are suddenly awake. Your heart is pounding, your adrenalin is pumping, and your muscles are tense. You find yourself sitting upright and can feel beads of sweat forming on your forehead. The silence is palpable. What just happened? Something snatched you unceremoniously out of oblivion and into a state of high alert. *Did I hear something?* you ponder. Then it happens: BUMP!

From somewhere in the darkness of your house you hear another noise—unmistakable evidence of an intruder on the premises. *Was that a collision into the dining room table, or a widescreen TV being dropped?* Your mind races. *Who is prowling around downstairs? Am I in danger?*

A primal decision has presented itself: fight or flight. Which one is your gut instinct when things go bump in the night? Some long for the day they get to put their martial arts skills to the test after hours of honing their slow-motion self-defense moves in a Krav Maga dojo. Others just want to curl into the fetal position, play possum, and hope the threat lumbers away.

Whatever your instinct, you certainly would feel at least slightly more confident if you had a weapon or two in your arsenal. The requisite investigation feels more manageable while gripping a golf club or Taser gun. That is what this book is meant to be for the intellectual investigation of intimidating biblical doctrines.

Let's be frank: There are some teachings in the Bible that are intimidating. Most sane Sunday school teachers don't devote their flannel graph lessons to passages that relate to eternal damnation, loss of rewards, church discipline, and demons. We don't grow up comfortable with these doctrines. Such species of teaching sound frightening and unhelpful.

Then there are the intellectually intimidating conundrums of free will and predestination, God's providence and concurrence, and various otherworldly terms relished by nerdy theological types and their ilk but largely overwhelming to most normal people who simply love the Lord and want to serve Him.

Why do some preachers and Bible teachers find the need to wander off the comfortable, pruned path of simplicity, and insist on exploring the deep woods of God's unfathomable wisdom? Why search the unsearchable? Why scrutinize the inscrutable? The answer is the same with regard to why you venture into the darkness of your home in pursuit of what went bump in the night: because it's there. Those who crouch into the fetal position don't repel burglars. Brave souls with golf clubs do.

When a doctrine goes bump in the church, our instinct might be to play intellectual possum and hope the mystery solves itself and the relevant Bible verses retreat peacefully back into obscurity. But a faithful student of Scripture is willing to face the mysterious and grapple with it.

What we want to do in this book is help put a few handy weapons in your arsenal. We want to arm you with the biblical texts and their explanations so that you have something to grab when you next encounter an intimidating doctrine. In short, we want to boost your confidence so that you are able to face the things that go bump in the church.

1

GRACE

*The Outrageous Implications of
the Most Delightful Truth Known to Man*

BYRON YAWN

Hell may seem a strange place to start a chapter on the doctrine of grace, but humor me for a moment. We'll go through hell to get to grace. This will eventually make sense (I hope). The following is now a rather infamous quote on the rather infamous subject of eternal punishment:

> I consider the concept of hell an outrageous doctrine. It's a bad doctrine which needs to be changed. How can Christians possibly project a deity of such cruelty and vindictiveness whose ways include inflicting everlasting torture upon His creatures, however sinful they may have been? Surely a God who would do such a thing is more nearly like Satan than like God, at least by any ordinary moral standards and by the Gospel itself. Surely the God and Father of our Lord Jesus Christ is no fiend. Torturing people without end is not what our God does. Everlasting torment is intolerable from a moral point of view because it makes God into a blood-thirsty monster who maintains an everlasting Auschwitz for victims whom He does not even allow the dignity to die. [1]

The first time ever I read this paragraph, I was stunned. The contempt in these words is beyond palpable. You end up putting your hand over your own mouth even though you didn't utter them. It's one of the more blatant disregards for the Word of God I've ever encountered. If the eternality of hell is real, then "God" is a "blood-thirsty monster"? Wow. And this from a Christian scholar. The expression of such guttural and sincere hatred for a biblical doctrine is rare. It makes you want to step aside and get clear of the lightning strike you're certain is en route. Who would ever dare to put such a thought in writing? Answer: someone who has realized the unbearable implications lying at the core of the doctrine of hell. A person who has stumbled upon the agonizing truth that makes it hell in the first place—unending punishment—and has chosen to deny it. It's not hell he objects to, but rather, the truth that makes it hell.

Regardless of our opinion of this individual, we can't deny that this liberal theologian grasps the doctrine of hell better than most evangelical Christians do. He understands the unbearable implication at the center of this devastating doctrine. And I should say that his sensitivities are rightly offended by it. The thought of human beings suffering physical torment for all eternity should make us cringe. Clearly, he gets this. Clearly, we don't. Otherwise we would react in similar fashion—without impugning the character of God or denying what He declared as true and just.

But if we actually grasped the implication regarding endless punishment, we'd tremble at the mention of hell. Furthermore, we too would think it "outrageous" because the idea of eternal torment for human beings would stick like a bone in our consciences. As it is, we toss the word *hell* around rather glibly, employing it as a synonym for *difficult*. The eternality of hell should be an unbearable doctrine that we circumspectly affirm as literal and true. Indeed, we should and must affirm hell as biblical, but we should never be complacent about the reality of hell. If we are, something is wrong with our soul.

As it turns out, the scholar I quoted above is angry at precisely the right thing. The aim of his objection is dead on. Ironically, his moral outrage and contempt has a sounder theological basis than our indifferent confession. He gets it. As is often the case, the opponent of a truth is better able to represent its essence than those who carelessly affirm it. I think as it concerns hell, we who confess it have no real idea what we are affirming in our confession.

A Delightfully Outrageous Truth

This then brings us to the discussion of grace. The gospel carries with it implications that border on outrageous to the mind of fallen and religious men. Wherever it is proclaimed, these implications follow with it. Those who realize the truth underneath the gospel push against it. That truth is *grace*—the unmerited favor of God poured out upon unworthy mankind. Grace is the good pleasure of God that causes Him to bestow His favor (in His Son) upon sinners without any regard to the ability of the person loved. Man, unable to save himself in any way, must depend upon the grace and mercy of God to act on his behalf. If man is not completely dependent upon the mercy of God in his salvation, then it is not of grace. Where our ability is present, grace is not present. Grace assumes inability. You cannot have one or the other. Either we are saved by grace, or we are not: "If it is by grace, it is no longer on the basis of works; otherwise grace would no longer be grace" (Romans 11:6).

If it is true that God saves by sovereign grace—and it is—then certain corollaries are also true. Those corollaries strike at tightly held assumptions and deeply imbedded prejudices in our nature. Ultimately, these are the items we so frequently debate. To be clear, when I speak of sovereign grace I am not referring to some specific historic confession or system of theology (such as Calvinism vs. Arminianism). I am referring to the reality that sinners are saved solely by the power of God. Finesse it all you want, debate it all you can, but the truth remains—if man is saved at all, it is God who saves him. There may be room for discussion around the edges, but when you get to the center, there you find it—salvation is by grace alone. This is an unmistakably *biblical* truth.

John 6:44—"No one can come to me unless the Father who sent me draws him."

Ephesians 2:4-9—"God, being rich in mercy, because of the great love with which he loved us, even when we were dead in our trespasses, made us alive together with Christ—by grace you have been saved—and raised us up with him and seated us with him in the heavenly places in Christ Jesus, so that in the coming ages he might show the immeasurable riches of his grace in kindness toward us in Christ Jesus. For by grace you have been saved through faith. And this is not your own doing; it is the gift of God, not a result of works, so that no one may boast."

Titus 3:4-7—"When the goodness and loving kindness of God our Savior appeared, he saved us, not because of works done by us in righteousness, but according to his own mercy, by the washing of regeneration and renewal of the Holy Spirit, whom he poured out on us richly through Jesus Christ our Savior, so that *being justified by his grace we might become heirs according to the hope of eternal life.*"

As you may know (and may have experienced firsthand), there is no subject that incites discussion as does the doctrine of sovereign grace. Just drop the word *election* at your next prayer meeting and see what happens. The reactions are usually strong in one of two directions—enthusiastic support, or enthusiastic objection. There is no real middle ground on the topic. The intensity of debate on this matter is due to the innumerable implications that ripple outward from it. God must act if man is to be saved? This raises all types of legitimate questions. The role of man in his own salvation. The place of faith. The necessity of belief. The destiny of those who do not believe. Again, all valid and important discussions. All of which are always resident within any mention of the gospel.

As with the doctrine of hell, those who most protest sovereign grace are often those who most clearly understand it and what it actually means. They are wrestling with the very premises at the heart of the gospel. Similarly, those who struggle with sovereign grace possess a better grasp of the doctrine than most casual adherents do. Too many of the implications of grace are outrageous and illogical. This is especially true with the religious person. Because a religious spirit is most concerned with man's participation in his reconciliation to God and grace denies such essential participation, many find themselves at an impasse. For grace denies the effect of religion. Therefore, grace appears as an outrageous and incompatible doctrine. Consequently, it receives an intense reaction.

That Nagging Need to Qualify Grace

This reaction was most evident in the ministry of the apostle Paul, who spent his life preaching and defending grace as the central theme of the gospel. He was unambiguous in his proclamation and defense. Paul's opponents got exactly the point he was making. It was not that they misunderstood what Paul was saying and needed it clarified. The two parties understood each other perfectly. They found his message intolerable because they realized what the gospel of grace meant for their lives and tradition. Though their objections were wrong, they were objecting over the right thing. They were not misunderstanding Paul. Rather, they understood and disagreed.

Wherever Paul preached the gospel, there was an outcry from opponents who realized exactly what Paul was declaring. The response to grace, when it is preached purely, is very predictable. You can hear him answering these predictable objections in a number of places. All of them in response to those who objected to this ridiculous notion of salvation by grace through faith.

Grace understood properly conflicts with both logic and religion. If you are secular, then it strikes you as being foolish. Why would God willingly offer His Son as a substitute for unworthy sinners? That's unjust. If you are religious, it strikes you as being irresponsible. If man is saved by grace and not merit, then men will abuse grace and live any way they want. Religion keeps man accountable. In Romans 6:1-5, Paul answered this very objection:

> What shall we say then? Are we to continue in sin that grace may abound? By no means! How can we who died to sin still live in it? Do you not know that all of us who have been baptized into Christ Jesus were baptized into his death? We were buried therefore with him by baptism into death, in order that, just as Christ was raised from the dead by the glory of the Father, we too might walk in newness of life. For if we have been united with him in a death like his, we shall certainly be united with him in a resurrection like his.

When grace is taught purely, it challenges both the secular and religious. The religious think it too easy. And the irreligious think it ridiculous. And on a certain level, they are right. Salvation by grace through faith is hard to comprehend and reconcile. It deserves debate. In other words, the opponents are on to something in their opposition. Grace does seem a dangerous doctrine to preach. That God would offer Himself for unworthy and corrupt rebels does seem illogical. Why would He do that? It seems unjust. If there isn't a part of you that is offended by all that God's grace entails, you probably aren't understanding it clearly.

This is why our conscience always wants to put footnotes on it. "God saves by grace…but man still must…" We can't leave it alone. We have an insatiable need to qualify it. Our resident ethicist will always raise objections. For when we grasp the matter of God's grace correctly, the implications are substantial. If people are not either objecting or rejoicing, then we are probably not presenting it correctly.

Paul Owns It All

One of Paul's clearest defenses of grace is found in the letter to the Galatians. In response to the many who were attaching all sorts of qualifiers to God's grace, Paul stepped up to defend the core truth—God saves by grace alone. It's here that he clearly lays out the many implications of this overwhelming reality. Essentially, he lets grace hang in the discussion and refuses to qualify it. Some taught that Law must be added to grace if any man is to be saved. Paul launched an arsenal in a defense of the true gospel for the Galatian Christians. As he did, he referred to an occasion in his own life to demonstrate how vigorously it must be defended:

> When Cephas came to Antioch, I opposed him to his face, because he stood condemned. For before certain men came from James, he was eating with the Gentiles; but when they came he drew back and separated himself, fearing the circumcision party. And the rest of the Jews acted hypocritically along with him, so that even Barnabas was led astray by their hypocrisy (Galatians 2:11-13).

Here's the context: Peter was sitting on the back porch of Gentile homes having a glass of wine and a ham sandwich. Enjoying the freedom of the gospel as an ethnic Jew. If we are saved by grace and works are no means of merit before God, then certain liberties follow. Peter—with his vision of a sheet (Acts 10:9-16)—was enjoying those liberties. When certain Jewish Christians showed up from Jerusalem preaching legalism, all that changed. Eventually Peter separated himself from his Gentile brothers out of fear of religious men. Paul noticed this and considered it a denial of the gospel itself. A submission to the religious requirements of men was a rejection of grace. If the likes of Peter and Barnabas could be carried off by such legalism, then certainly others can. Paul called it what it was—*hypocrisy.*

> When I saw that their conduct was not in step with *the truth of the gospel,* I said to Cephas before them all, "If you, though a Jew, live like a Gentile and not like a Jew, how can you force the Gentiles to live like Jews?" (verse 14).

When Paul realized what was happening, he confronted Peter to his face. That's crazy boldness! He exposed his hypocrisy. He literally called him out. Peter and Barnabas were shrinking from what Paul describes as "the truth of the gospel." In other words, Paul embraced all the implications of grace, which his two partners were now denying by their actions. Make no mistake—the one truth that so offended the legalistic mob was *grace*. That reality is at the center of the gospel which either offends or liberates. Paul stepped right up and owned it with all of its implications. Without qualification. Paul knew, as did his opponents, you could not have both law and grace. It is always an either/or proposition. It is never both/and. If you insert one, you naturally banish the other.

From here on, Paul owned every implication of the "truth of the gospel" his opponents expected him to shrink from. He put them all out on the table and refused to hide from a single one of them. He was more than comfortable with the tension it created. Everything we ever feel the need to qualify he let rest there awkwardly on the consciences of his opponents. Paul would not give in to the pressure. As he mentioned previously, "We did not yield in submission even for a moment, so that the truth of the gospel might be preserved for you" (Galatians 2:5). And so he laid out every thorny little implication of grace that he could think of:

> We are Jews by nature, and not sinners from among the Gentiles; nevertheless knowing that a man is not justified by the works of the Law but through faith in Christ Jesus, even we have believed in Christ Jesus, so that we may be justified by faith in Christ and not by the works of the Law; since by the works of the Law shall no flesh be justified. But if, while seeking to be justified in Christ, we ourselves have also been found sinners, is Christ then a minister of sin? May it never be! For if I rebuild what I have once destroyed, I prove myself to be a transgressor. For through the Law I died to the Law, that I might live to God. I have been crucified with Christ; and it is no longer I who live, but Christ lives in me; and the life which I now live in the flesh I live by faith in the Son of God, who loved me and gave Himself up for me. I do not nullify the grace of God, for if righteousness comes through the Law, then Christ died needlessly (verses 15-21 NASB).

The Implications of Grace

1. *If grace is true, then you are no better before God than the worst person you can imagine.*

This is hard for us to take, but it has to be true if grace is real. This is what Paul is getting at when he wrote, "We are Jews by nature and not sinners from among the Gentiles" (2:15 NASB). "Sinners among the Gentiles" is code for "those" people. You know, the really sinful people. The ones washing their boats on Sunday as you are making your way to church. Regardless of the moral distinction Paul's Jewish brothers may have maintained between themselves and the Gentiles, they were no closer to pleasing God. This is exactly what Paul goes on to explain in the rest of the passage.

We are all saved by the mercy of God. That statement immediately implies that all are in need of God's mercy. Which implies that we are all helpless. We may compare ourselves to others and think ourselves more deserving of God's mercy—especially in comparison to a particularly wicked person. But grace says otherwise. You don't deserve mercy. You receive it. This has to be true if the gospel is real. "By grace" implies the absence of any personal claims of worthiness. We are saved in the same manner as the rest of the sinners on this planet are—by faith in the righteous life of another. Self-righteousness is not just a bad attitude toward other people; it is a denial of the gospel. It assumes there's something in us that God finds pleasing. According to grace, you should view yourself as bad or worse than the worst person you can imagine. And from here you can rightly marvel at God's love toward you in Christ. As Paul said in Romans 2:11-12, "God shows no partiality. For all who have sinned without the law will also perish without the law, and all who have sinned under the law will be judged by the law."

2. *If grace is true, God is not impressed with our good works.*

Our works merit us nothing before God. In our hearts we know this is true. Our good works do nothing to secure our position in Christ. Our works are not the object of our faith. Our faith is in the object of the work of Christ. Our good works are the grateful response to the love of God and not the cause of it. Faith in the gospel produces good works in the life of the believer, not the other way around.

But, nonetheless, we seem to constantly measure our standing before God by a comparison of ourselves to other people. Or we measure other people against our lives. We betray grace when we do because we are trusting in our works for salvation. We assume that our maturity, obedience, or knowledge of the Bible puts us at an advantage over others. But no one is saved by works. Before or after salvation.

> We know that a person is not justified by the works of the law but through faith in Jesus Christ, so we also have believed in Christ Jesus, in order to be justified by faith in Christ and not by works of the law; because by works of the law no one will be justified (Galatians 2:16 NASB).

"So we" is a strong statement. Paul means the Jews. The most moral people on the face of the earth had to turn from their good deeds and place their faith in the good deeds of another. The implication is brutal for the self-righteous. What you do does not affect your standing before God. God saved you despite your failure to be good enough. You have been covered in an alien righteousness by faith. It lies outside of you. Your deeds or lack thereof cannot improve or diminish your standing before God, even after salvation.

"But," someone will say, "God does expect a changed life." And there comes the qualifier. Yes, indeed He does. In fact, Paul went on to confront any who denied the necessity of change.

> If, while seeking to be justified in Christ, we ourselves have also been found sinners, is Christ then a minister of sin? May it never be! For if I rebuild what I have once destroyed, I prove myself to be a transgressor (verses 17-18 NASB).

Basically, anyone who abuses grace and continues in a life of unrepentant sin was never saved in the first place. In a true believer, there is change on a very deep level. But that change is caused and effected by the power of God and not us. We are not the cause of our changed life.

Our changed life is the cause of change. Even our good works, which are *really* ours, originate from God: "We are his workmanship, created in Christ Jesus for good works, which God prepared beforehand, that we should walk in them" (Ephesians 2:10).

The real question is this: Do you think your changed life is the cause or result of your salvation? Honestly, depending on what state of mind we are in, our answer varies. But, regardless, even our good works result from God's grace and are not for the purpose of earning grace. We have a hard time getting away from this idea. We have a tendency to read our works into everything.

For example: "But God shows his love for us in that while we were still sinners, Christ died for us *on the condition that after a reasonable length of time we would be the kind of people no one would ever have to die for in the first place. Otherwise, the deal is off.*"

3. *If grace is true, then I am no longer held responsible for my violations of the Law of God.*

"For through the Law I died to the Law, so that I might live to God" (Galatians 2:19 NASB). The Law had tried and condemned Paul. He was totally guilty and deserving of death. It was hard for a dedicated Jewish man to admit such great failure, but Paul was more than happy to admit it. Admitting it was his freedom. When he finally saw the holy standard of God, he knew his own righteousness amounted to a pile of dung. He would suffer hell's torment if he swung out into eternity trusting his own works. Christ substituted Himself for Paul and took on his penalty. When Christ died, Paul died. When Christ was raised, Paul was raised.

By trusting in the work of Christ—rather than his own—Paul survived the death penalty executed by the Law. The punishment for his sins had been satisfied in Christ's atoning death. The righteous standard of God in the Law was satisfied in the righteous life of Christ. Every sin Paul would ever commit was paid for. He could not be condemned.

> There is therefore now no condemnation for those who are in Christ Jesus. For the law of the Spirit of life has set you

free in Christ Jesus from the law of sin and death. For God has done what the law, weakened by the flesh, could not do. By sending his own Son in the likeness of sinful flesh and for sin, he condemned sin in the flesh, in order that the righteous requirement of the law might be fulfilled in us, who walk not according to the flesh but according to the Spirit (Romans 8:1-4).

We who are in Christ no longer live under the penalty of the Law. We died by and to the Law in Christ. We will never suffer the consequences for our sins—past, present, and future. Why? Because the fullest penalty the Law had to offer—death—was carried out in our substitute. This penalty is paid for. Christ was put to death, and we lived to tell about it. Because of grace, we will never suffer the penalty for our sins.

We struggle with this implication most. As well we should. If we don't, we're not getting it. It is the one that gets down to the core of most people's concern. This is where grace starts sounding irresponsible and reckless. If we will never be held responsible for our sins, doesn't that mean we can live any way that we want? Is this not a license for sin? How can we control people's behavior if they think they can get away with any behavior they choose? We may understand where the concern is coming from, but we must refuse to qualify it. If we choose to qualify it, then we are, in essence, denying the net effect of the work of Christ on the cross. We are free from the penalty of the Law because He died.

Paul answered this objection frequently because it was usually the first objection raised: "You can't tell people that. They'll live like hell on their way to heaven!" But Paul's opponents missed the big picture. It wasn't only that grace corrected one's legal standing before God (justification through faith); it first created a new disposition (regeneration by grace). It is grace that allows us to love God and gives us a desire to please Him in the first place. Our desire to please God is the result of Christ having pleased Him. We are set free to obey because Christ perfectly obeyed.

You were called to freedom, brothers. Only do not use your freedom as an opportunity for the flesh, but through love serve one another. For the whole law is fulfilled in one word: "You shall love your neighbor as yourself." But if you bite and devour one another, watch out that you are not consumed by one another. But I say, walk by the Spirit, and you will not gratify the desires of the flesh (Galatians 5:13-16).

Our obedience is the result of inner transformation by the Spirit's power and not anything that we do.

4. *If grace is true, then the whole of our Christian existence is dependent on it, not just the beginning.*

Look back at Galatians 2:20: "I have been crucified with Christ. It is no longer I who live, but Christ who lives in me. And the life I now live in the flesh I live by faith in the Son of God, who loved me and gave himself for me."

This verse has been misplaced and misunderstood by countless Christians over the years. We generally apply it as a motivation to keep on living the Christian life. As if Paul were inspiring us to keep pushing on in our Christian experience. But actually it's more a theological statement than a practical one. He wasn't encouraging us to keep *moving*. He was encouraging us to keep *believing*. Paul was making a declarative break from his previous way of life. This is a treatise against a works-based existence.

Before Christ, it was Paul who "lived" for Paul. His life in the "flesh," as he calls it, was dedicated to intensive self-improvement and a commitment to change. In other words, he lived exactly like his opponents were encouraging others to live—according to works. But he no longer lived this way. The old Paul and his former way of life were put to death in Christ. His life now was lived by faith in the "Son of God, who loved me, and gave himself for me." Every day was a day dependent on grace. Anything Paul did or was resulted from his unrelenting focus on the person and work of Jesus Christ. It was not him, but Christ coming through him.

You can see why this is immediately disruptive to the way we normally live our Christian life. We usually view the gospel as the mere entry point of Christianity. We are saved by grace, and then we take it from there. God gets us in, and then we get ourselves the rest of the way. The gospel and grace are usually minimized in our ongoing spiritual growth. We rarely take note of them along the way in our Christian life experience. Paul, by contrast, expressed the exact opposite reality in his own life. Christ's work was not merely the entry point; it was the entire course. The life he lived was lived "by faith in the Son of God" and not in his works.

We are just as dependent on God's grace today as we were on the day we became Christians. It is Christ who lives in us. It is He who makes it all possible.

INSIGHTS FROM THE PAST

If you take away the Grace of God from the Gospel you have extracted from it its very life-blood and there is nothing left worth preaching, worth believing, or worth contending for. Grace is the soul of the Gospel—without it the Gospel is dead. Grace is the music of the Gospel—without it the Gospel is silent as to all comfort.

God deals with sinful men upon the footing of pure mercy—finding them guilty and condemned, He gives free pardons, altogether irrespective of past character, or of any good works which may be foreseen. Moved only by pity, He devises a plan for their rescue from sin and its consequences—a plan in which Grace is the leading feature.

Out of free favor He has provided, in the death of His dear Son, an atonement by means of which His mercy can be justly bestowed. He accepts all those who place their trust in this Atonement, selecting faith as the way of salvation, that it may be all of Grace. In this He acts, from a motive found within Himself, and not because of any reason found in the sinner's conduct—past, present, or future. I tried to show that this Grace of God flows towards the sinner from of old and begins its operations upon him when there is nothing good in him—it works in him that which is good and acceptable—and continues so to work in him till the deed of Grace is complete and the Believer is received up into the glory for which he is made meet.

Grace commences to save and it perseveres till all is done. From first to last, from the "A" to the "Z" of the heavenly alphabet, everything in salvation is of Grace and Grace alone! All is of free favor, nothing of merit. "By Grace are you saved through faith; and that not of yourselves; it is the gift of God." "So then it is not of him that wills, nor of him that runs, but of God that shows mercy." No sooner is this doctrine set forth in a clear light than men begin to quibble with it. It is the target for all carnal logic to shoot at. Unrenewed minds never liked it and they never will—it is too humbling to human pride, making light of the nobility of human nature. That men are to be saved by Divine charity; that they must, as condemned criminals, receive pardon by the exercise of the royal prerogative or else perish in their sins is a teaching which they cannot endure!

Charles Haddon Spurgeon, "The Doctrines of Grace Do Not Lead to Sin,"
preached at Exeter Hall on August 19, 1883

2

SIN

The Hairy Wart on the Witch's Nose

MIKE ABENDROTH

As the witches in Shakespeare's *Macbeth* churn their smoldering cauldron, the second witch delivers the famous recipe for her nefarious spell:

> Eye of newt, and toe of frog,
> Wool of bat, and tongue of dog,
> Adder's fork, and blind-worm's sting,
> Lizard's leg, and howlet's wing—
> For a charm of powerful trouble,
> Like a hell-broth boil and bubble. [1]

While I am not exactly sure of the meaning of every ingredient ("eye of newt" is an herb, not an optical orb of a salamander, and "howlet" is a cool, poetic name for an owl), I do know that it must have been an ultra-noxious potion (where is some air freshener when you need it?).

Sadly, due to the torrential flood of man-centered, psychological influences in our world, the ultimate reason and explanation for man's predicament is not found anywhere near the vicinity of the Garden of Eden. Society's spiritual GPS needs updating. *Sin* is the new "s" word in our culture from the halls of the universities to the front-page news splashes of the media. Is anyone responsible for anything anymore? Is there any blame to go around? I would not be shocked if modern witches—"white witches," of course—were to brew an up-to-the-minute Freudian potion perfectly concocted to avoid all human responsibility. A pinch of duck and a dash of jive added for good measure. Can't you just hear the contemporary Shakespearean characters dolefully harmonize, "Eye of disease, and toe of illness, tongue of ailment, Adder's syndrome, howlet's sickness, unwellness of bat, disorder of blindworm, and lizard's codependency?" Yuck. Around our house, when people try to avoid taking personal responsibility for their actions, we just call the figurative broth "pass the buck" soup. Salt to taste. Tabasco not necessary. Teflon coated.

The purpose of this chapter is not to dissect mental illnesses or psychotic diseases. Rather, it will attempt to simply acknowledge sin for what it is so that you can confess it as sin and receive God's forgiveness and mercy. Ever hear of a syndrome being forgiven? A disease? A malady? No. Sins are ultimately perpetrated against a holy God who cannot tolerate sin, and the only hope of breaking away from sin lies in the free forgiveness provided by Jesus Christ Himself. Sovereign forgiveness. Granted by the One whom you sinned against. Admitting sin might seem or feel counterintuitive, yet owning up to your sin is the most liberating thing that can ever occur to you. Literally.

The Pathology of Blame

The first time I saw an autopsy performed on a human (a dead one, of course), it was pretty difficult to sleep for a few nights afterward—even though I had witnessed hundreds of surgeries performed on live humans when I was working in the operating room. The surgeons, with few exceptions, sutured up the patients and the anesthesiologists woke them up. Within days the recovered patients took off their green hospital gowns and exchanged them for their jeans and went home.

But the scene in morgues is more final. More ultimate. The doctor performing the autopsy pulled back the skin on the scalp to get to the brain. He needed a sample. He opened up the abdomen and made some large incisions so that he could get some cross-sections of the liver. The physician was searching, in Columbo-like fashion, for the cause of death. Why did this person die? Mere metal scalpels, no matter how brilliant the surgeon, cannot dissect the human soul. But if a surgeon could do that, he would come face-to-face with a brutally incriminating fact: People sin because they want to sin, and their sins wreak havoc upon themselves, everyone around them, and are ultimately perpetrated against God.

Can you determine the common denominator in the following litany of excuses?

"I am only human."

"To err is human."

"God made me this way."

"God doesn't make junk."

"I was born this way."

"I was born gay."

Each excuse is meticulously fabricated and molded to avoid incrimination and judgment, while reflecting away personal responsibility and pinning the blame elsewhere. Tail, meet donkey. Who, then, is the recipient of the blame? It is ultimately directed toward God Himself. Such sin-deflection talk tries to excuse volitional behavior by blaming God, the Holy One, Himself. The twisted logic goes something like this: "After all, if the Creator makes something, it ought to do what it is supposed to do." But the proponents of this logic, as we used to say as children, "accidentally on purpose" forget Ecclesiastes 7:29, which declares, "See, this alone I found, that God made man upright, but they have sought out many schemes." In other words, God made Adam and Eve perfect in the Garden, but because of man's own rebellion, Adam—and all his children—are now fallen, depraved, and sin-riddled. God did not create the original man and woman as sinful beings. They were not made sinners on the day they were created. They became sinners by their own doing.

We should not be surprised, because blaming God is nothing new. Even Homer, as he described God speaking in heaven, wrote, "Zeus now addressed the immortals. 'What a lamentable thing it is that men should blame the gods and regard us as the source of their troubles when it is their own wickedness that brings them sufferings worse than any which destiny allots them!'" [2]

James, the half brother of Jesus, wrote some words that should forever stifle the censure of God by wrongfully blaming Him for human sin. The apostle set the record straight when he said:

> Let no one say when he is tempted, "I am being tempted by God," for God cannot be tempted with evil, and he himself tempts no one. But each person is tempted when he is lured and enticed by his own desire. Then desire when it has conceived gives birth to sin, and sin when it is fully grown brings forth death. Do not be deceived, my beloved brothers (James 1:13-16).

James wanted his readers to never fall into attributing any blame to God, no matter how difficult the situation. He taught that temptation is never from God. All accusations, direct or indirect, that indict God are to be abandoned as quickly as a pilot pulls his escape hatch lever. A direct charge against God sounds like Adam in Genesis 3:12: "The woman whom you gave to be with me, she gave me fruit of the tree, and I ate." And an indirect charge sounds like Eve in Genesis 3:13: "Then the LORD God said to the woman, 'What is this that you have done?' The woman said, 'The serpent deceived me, and I ate.'" Could anything trumpet "men and women are depraved" more loudly than blaming God for wrongdoing in the hopes of escaping personal responsibility?

Among the more nuanced, subtle methods of finding fault with God is to cloak transgressions behind the veil of heredity ("my Italian temper"), the shroud of environment ("my dysfunctional family"), or the wry mantle of "Satan made me do it" (yes, I watched Flip Wilson as a child). Rationalizations, no matter what the apparent merit might initially and falsely portray, are pointless and unsuccessful attempts to wriggle out of the straitjacket of individual sin. "The test God gave me was too hard!" rings hollow in light of James's words.

James, inspired by the Holy Spirit, declared that God never tempts people. God's upright character is at stake, and His holiness and righteousness will never allow Him to breach His perfections. Instead of tempting people, "He leads me in paths of righteousness for his name's sake" (Psalm 23:3). God never needs us to forgive Him because He is impeccable and unsullied. God does try and test people as He did Abraham, Job, and Hezekiah, although He tests them with pure motives and no wicked intentions.

Then where does the real culpability lie for sin? Man is induced to sin not by any external force, but from the inside. To quote one of my former seminary professors, "You made you do sin." James 1:14 makes it clear "each person is tempted when he is lured and enticed by his own desire." Sinful desire tries to drag people away like a tiger would haul off its prey, so beware the hook that is hidden beneath the bait of lust and desire. Jesus was clear when He exposed the true source of every evil and wicked defilement:

> He said to them, "Then are you also without understanding? Do you not see that whatever goes into a person from outside cannot defile him, since it enters not his heart but his stomach, and is expelled?" (Thus he declared all foods clean.) And he said, "What comes out of a person is what defiles him. For from within, out of the heart of man, come evil thoughts, sexual immorality, theft, murder, adultery, coveting, wickedness, deceit, sensuality, envy, slander, pride, foolishness. All these evil things come from within, and they defile a person" (Mark 7:18-23).

A biblical definition of sin can help us build a scaffold of support against erroneous thinking about God. The Westminster Shorter Catechism defines sin as "any want of conformity unto or transgression of the law of God." Sin, in other words, is always first and foremost against God Himself. Sin might additionally be perpetrated against other people, but it is primarily against God. David sinned against Bathsheba (adultery), Uriah (murder), and the nation of Israel, but He correctly lamented, "Against you, you only, have I sinned and done what is evil in your sight" (Psalm 51:4). Never turn your sin, which you have ultimately committed against God, into a missile aimed at blaming God. God does not sin. He has no need of forgiveness. Stop blaming Him.

Puritan Jeremiah Burroughs carefully articulated the truth that should be riveted to our minds:

> The chief of all is the humiliation of the soul for sin as it is against God. Then is the heart humbled rightly for sin when it apprehends how, by sin, the soul has been against the infinite, glorious First-Being of all things. All other humiliations in the world are not sufficient without this. For it is not deep enough. There can be no humiliation deep enough unless the soul is humbled for sin because it has sinned against God.[3]

Shortly after I married my wife, Kim, my full depravity snarled. The clothes dresser could not defend itself. Although not a Christian at the time, I was still a full-grown man. The scenario: marital disagreement. Mike thinking and acting like brat. *Baby* would be a more fitting word than *brat. Infant.* Mike raised voice and razed the cheap dresser. Ruined. Think Humpty Dumpty. It was at that moment that I thought, "I don't have an anger problem; I *am* the problem."

You see, anger problems can be solved by those specializing in *anger management* (two words that don't seem to make sense together, except in our society). The Lord "let me in" on my secret—every person's secret: We are all wicked in the very core of our being. Our minds, emotions, and will are all sin-stained and theologically warped. I am the problem. I am sinful. Sin was bursting forth, and its origin was from within!

For clarity's sake, sin is not something we have. Sin is more than what we do or don't do. Sin(ful) is something we *are.* I did not need "help" with my anger; I needed to be rescued by a Substitute. Salvation was priority number one (anger was a symptom of my soul's need). Not only salvation from the wrath of the Lord Jesus (which is certainly needed), but also salvation from my sinful self. Thankfully, the Lord God saved me from my sinfulness a few short months later. And we now have wooden dressers that are very solid. Not because I might attempt to splinter them into many pieces, but because we inherited them from Grandma.

As pride-shattering as it was to recognize my own wretchedness, it was the dawning of my spiritual awakening. God used my infantile outburst to force me to own my sinfulness. What I meant for evil, God meant for good. Specifically, God taught me, "Whoever conceals his transgressions will not prosper, but he who confesses and forsakes them will obtain mercy" (Proverbs 28:13).

Read that verse again and let its message sink in. Here is a different translation to assist you: "He that covereth his transgressions shall not prosper: But whoso confesseth and forsaketh them shall obtain mercy" (ASV).

When we try to create a smoke screen around our sins for the sake of diverting God's attention, it only leads to the chastening hand of God. Wearing camouflage at night might seem wise, but if a sniper has night-vision goggles or scopes, we are still vulnerable. How much more can God see past and through our sin disguises! Asylum from God's gaze is impossible. Haven from God's all-seeing omniscience is as irrational as sin itself. Sin makes stupid. Shelter is found only through agreeing with God about the sin. Refuge is via confession. Forgiveness is found when you agree with God and turn from your sin (or sins).

The writer of Proverbs unveils the absolute gold mine of confessing and forsaking sin—that is, the obtaining of mercy. The English word *mercy* has its origin in the English word for *womb*. So when *mercy* is used to translate its Old Testament Hebrew equivalent, it communicates in a picturesque way the idea of pity from a superior one, such as the pity of a tender mother for her baby. Or in this case, pity from God, the superior One. When used in a context dealing with sin or transgression, the term *mercy* highlights the grace of a forgiving God. The Creator offers relief, so stop running like a fugitive! And flee to God with your confession.

Recalling the truth of Proverbs 28:13, do you desire the Lord's...

Compassion or coldness?

Benevolence or chastisement?

Munificence or miserliness?

Bounty or scarcity?

Abundance or reprimand?

Grace or punishment?

Mercy or severity?

Then confess your sin. Run to the Savior of sinners. What is the ultimate ground for the mercy and grace of forgiveness? Some teach it is baptism. Others proclaim it is moral living. The Bible exclusively declares that Jesus died a vicarious death in the place of sinners just like you and me. Mercy can occur only because of the substitutionary atonement of Jesus Christ. John the apostle marries confession of sin and forgiveness in his first epistle:

> If we say we have no sin, we deceive ourselves, and the truth is not in us. If we confess our sins, he is faithful and just to forgive us our sins and to cleanse us from all unrighteousness. If we say we have not sinned, we make him a liar, and his word is not in us. My little children, I am writing these things to you so that you may not sin. But if anyone does sin, we have an advocate with the Father, Jesus Christ the righteous. He is the propitiation for our sins, and not for ours only but also for the sins of the whole world (1 John 1:8–2:2).

What God has joined together—namely, confession and forgiveness—let no man tear asunder.

Instead of trying to hide your sin in some secret compartment deep within, open up the front door to your life and let the light of forgiveness expose it. And do so with confidence in the Bible and Christ's finished work at Calvary. When Christians sin, they have someone who will stand in their defense. John is painting brush strokes of a courtroom setting in which Jesus Christ is our lawyer, representing us before the court of God. Jesus is our helper when we sin. He helps by dying a wrath-bearing death (propitiation) and by being our righteousness. Christ's active intercession guarantees that our sins do not eternally debar us from God's holy heaven. Fellowship with God is a certainty for sinners with an advocate, the Advocate Jesus.

What you should never say when you sin (against God or others): "Sorry."

"I am sorry."

"I am sorry if you were hurt."

"I apologize."

"I apologize if you took my words the wrong way."

What is the common denominator in these less-than-full confessions? No ownership. No realization of the offense committed. When you stub someone's toe by accident, you can rightfully say, "I am sorry." But when you sin, saying "I am sorry" does not approach biblical confession, agreement, and ownership. Instead, you need to say, "God, I have clearly and purposely sinned against You and Your holy law. I agree what I did was sinful, and I humbly ask You to forgive me of this transgression based upon Your Son's redemptive work on my behalf." God knows all about each sin you commit; there is no use trying to hide from an omnipresent, omniscient God.

The link between the confession of sin and the receiving of God's mercy is also found in Psalm 51. The superscript (title) at the beginning of the psalm reads, "To the choirmaster. A Psalm of David, when Nathan the prophet went to him, after he had gone in to Bathsheba." David was finished running from his sins. The Hound of Heaven had tracked him down through the prophet Nathan. David was convicted. He was undone. He had nowhere else to run, so he ran to the shelter of God, who is by nature a saving and forgiving God.

Notice how David put an end to many months of dodging ownership. He no longer blamed anyone or anything else. By God's grace, David took responsibility for his sin and poured out his heart in full acknowledgment of what he had done wrong. Learn from David's example:

> Have mercy on me, O God, according to your steadfast love; according to your abundant mercy blot out my transgressions. Wash me thoroughly from my iniquity, and cleanse me from my sin! (Psalm 51:1-2).

The degree of heinousness regarding David's sin with Bathsheba can only be trumped by the degree of the mercy and grace of God mediated through the death of the Son of David, Jesus Christ.

What About You?

Are you blaming anyone or anything for your own sins? Never accuse God of giving us rules that are too hard to obey. Don't fall into the trap of thinking *God, You just don't understand my situation.* Halt all reasoning that either directly or indirectly accuses God. And stop blaming others for your actions and attitudes. Own up. Man up. Woman up. And look up. Look up to the heavens and call out to God, the Savior. Forgiveness and mercy are available. What is the best course of action, especially if you want mercy, grace, and a clean conscience? Answer: confession, admission, and fleeing to the cross of the Savior, Jesus Christ.

God's generosity is available to you. Admit your unworthiness and grab, by faith, the worthy Savior. R.L. Wheeler's often-quoted paragraph highlights the greatness of Jesus Christ and how receptive He is to those who turn from their sin, run from blaming others, and trust in the work He did on their behalf:

> If I had the wisdom of Solomon, the patience of John, the meekness of Moses, the strength of Samson, the obedience of Abraham, the compassion of Joseph, the tears of Jeremiah, the poetic skill of David, the prophetic voice of Elijah, the courage of Daniel, the greatness of John the Baptist, the endurance and love of Paul, I would still need redemption through Christ's blood, the forgiveness of sin. [4]

When we were children, we loved to play board games. We eventually outgrew Chutes and Ladders and moved to games like Risk or Stratego. Ask the Lord to help you grow out of the "blame game" and move toward confession and repentance. There is no risk involved, only life eternal and sweet communion with the Lord.

////////////////// INSIGHTS FROM THE PAST //////////////////

But what, then, is original sin? According to the Apostle it is not only the lack of a good quality in the will, nor merely the loss of man's righteousness and ability. It is rather the loss of all his powers of body and soul, of his whole outward and inward perfections. In addition to this, it is his inclination to all that is evil, his aversion against that which is good, his antipathy against light and wisdom, his love for error and darkness, his flight from and his loathing of good works, and his seeking after that which is sinful. Thus we read in Psalm 14:3: "They are all gone aside, they are all together become filthy; there is none that doeth good, no, not one"; and in Genesis 8:21: "The imagination of man's heart is evil from his youth." Actual sins essentially consist in this that they come from out of us, as the Lord says in Matthew 15:19: "Out of the heart proceed evil thoughts, murders, adulteries, fornications, thefts, false witness, blasphemies." But original sin enters into us; we do not commit it, but we suffer it. We are sinners because we are the sons of a sinner. A sinner can beget only a sinner, who is like him.

Martin Luther, *Commentary on Romans*,
trans. J. Theodore Mueller (Grand Rapids: Zondervan, 1954), 95

3

FREEDOM OF THE WILL

The Five-Finger Death Punch of Theology

BYRON YAWN

At some point in nearly every debate about "who does what" in salvation a certain phrase is dropped that strikes fear into the hearts of all involved: "I believe men have free will." Like a triple-dog dare issued on a schoolyard, people back up to give it space. Free will is an intensely polarizing subject. It is more often put forward as a theological trump card against Calvinism than any other concept. "More moderate" theological constructs may take refuge within its walls. For many it is the final and insurmountable fallback defense against the logical minions of Reformed theology. Free will is the mother of all theological comebacks.

In the realm of debate the issuance of free will is a classic *emotional appeal* intended to play upon the sympathies of the listener. For certain, it is palpable. Within this discussion it is the emotional equivalent of setting a basket of puppies in front of an oncoming and uncaring steamroller of hard determinism. Who would dare advance against a reality as noble as man's capacity to freely choose and love God? Who would dare trample over the treasured premises that underlie free will?

Free will as a doctrine (people have the capacity to choose God) is intended to protect the quality of love between God and sinner. If it is not a free choice, it cannot be real love. If it is not real love, it was not a real choice. This sequence eventually leads to the five-finger death punch of theological debate: "Are we just a bunch of robots?" Free will and its corollaries pin the opponent down in an inescapable contradiction between sincere love and unfeeling predestination. How can one possibly object to free will without appearing as the Ebenezer Scrooge of theology? Debate over, right? Not hardly. Bah humbug!

When that moment comes—and people are expecting you to hand over your doctrinal pink slip—simply say the following: "No one believes in free will. Not even you. You simply haven't thought about what you're saying." Then sit back and enjoy the look on your friend's face as you move the goalposts of the debate to an undisclosed location. He won't see it coming. I love that moment. I realize this sounds presumptuous and arrogant ("Byron, how can you possibly know what someone is thinking?"), but it's true. Those who refer to free will in such a context usually haven't thought through the concept. If they understood it properly, they would not talk of it the way they do. There is no basket of puppies. There is no steamroller. It's a false dilemma.

Fact is, free will is one of the more notorious misnomers in church history. Most Christians, even those who hold to it, misunderstand it. This is relatively easy to prove. Let me explain. You know the expression, "She eats like a bird"? Many assume it's the same as saying something like, "She's rail thin and barely eats anything." We intend it as a compliment. But birds actually eat as much as half their body weight on a daily basis. They are the virtual "pigs" of the sky. That means the expression is *not* a compliment. Point is, we think we're saying one thing when we are actually saying the exact opposite. We simply don't understand what we are talking about. If we did, we'd stop saying certain things.

It's the same way with "I believe men have free will." Those who say it think they are defending the essence of grace and the gospel. But they are actually denying it. They haven't thought through the implications of what they're saying.

No one, not even secular philosophers, truly believes in the freedom of the will. Technically speaking, freedom of the will is an impossibility. You need only to consider the premise for a moment. The basic idea behind the expression "freedom of the will" is the belief that the human will is uninfluenced by anything other than itself. When it comes to freedom of the will, no external circumstance is involved. The will is free. It is self-determined. It is moved purely by its own inclinations. Which ultimately means your will is not inclined to make any decision based on a preference or the surrounding environment. It is uninfluenced. Therefore, it is "free" to choose whatever it desires without consideration of any particular object or its quality. In fact, it has to be this way for free will to actually exist. Otherwise, if it's not uninfluenced, some other force would have sway over the will. It would not be free.

If your will is truly free, it simply chooses without concern for any given object. If it faces two objects, it may choose either without partiality. Philosophers and theologians refer to this as the Law of Contrary Choice. In order for the will to be free (and a choice to be legitimate) it must have the opportunity to refuse, or to choose between two objects without a preference for either.

Imagine you have two bowls before you. One is full of your favorite flavor of ice cream ("favorite" is impossible according to free will, but we'll go with it anyway). The other is full of cottage cheese. According to the premise of free will, you must not only be able to choose either, but you must also be able to desire them equally. Of course, this would never happen. This scenario is a logical absurdity. So is free will in the truest sense of the concept. You will have a preference. You can't avoid having one. There's no way you could. Even if you've never tasted either, something will influence your decision. You will prefer one more than the other and choose it based on your preference. In this sense, your will is not absolutely free. Every choice we make is partly determined by something outside of our will. It's the way the universe is designed.

Not convinced? Here's another example. Most everyone has a certain food they don't like. Broccoli is an easy target here. Some people can't tolerate broccoli. When you ask them why, they usually answer something like, "I don't know. I can't stand it." If you press them they may say, "I don't like the taste" or "I don't like the texture." That leads to another question to ask them: "But why don't you like the taste?" It sounds ridiculous, I know, but it gets directly to the issue at hand. It is a question we don't usually think to ask but should. The answer is very predictable: "I don't know. I simply don't like the taste of broccoli."

It's here that you begin to see the demise of free will. If a person doesn't like broccoli and cannot explain why, it clearly means his will is subject to something he cannot understand or control. In this sense, his will is not free. If it were, he could like broccoli and he could choose to like it.

There are countless unseen forces affecting our wills every day. Basically freedom of the will does not exist in the way we think it does. When we say "I believe men have free will," we cannot possibly mean it. We are suggesting something in this statement we don't intend, something we don't actually believe.

Usually what we're really trying to get at when we mention free will is the logical tension that exists between God's sovereignty and human agency. Ultimately, this is a much better way of framing of the real issue. How do the sovereignty of God and human agency co-exist? How can we truly make choices if God determines everything that happens? The question isn't Do we have free will? Rather it's Are we actually *moral agents*?

Is there really a significant difference between the concepts of *free will* and *free agency*? Indeed there is. And the distinction is very important in this discussion. The former is a discussion about the effects of sin on the human will. The latter is a discussion about the workings of human existence in light of the reality of God's nature. Free will is a very specific discussion about the role man plays in his own salvation. Does God choose man, or does man choose God, or is it both? Can man, of his own free will, bring himself to God? The way people answer this particular question ultimately determines the theological school of thought they fall under. We'll eventually get to this question, but suffice it to say, barrels of ink have been spilled over this particular issue.

By contrast, the matter of *free agency* is more general. It involves the same basic conflict between sovereignty and human choices, but is broader in scope. *Free agency* is about how the choices we make every day and the sovereignty of God relate to one another. It is not concerned with whether you chose God in salvation as much as it is with whether you chose the shirt you're wearing. In reality, the issue of free agency is around us all the time. It's basic to our existence as human beings endowed with self-awareness. It relates to almost any-thing and everything we experience. Do we actually make choices as human agents? Or is God sovereign over our choices? Does He deter-mine what we do? Or do we actually do it? Did we choose to wear the clothes we have on, or did God ordain it? How does our human agency work in light of God's sovereignty? All legitimate questions.

Some would argue that the two realities—sovereignty and human agency—cannot co-exist. They are incompatible concepts. Those who hold this view are often referred to as *incompatibilists*. From their per-spective, absolute sovereignty and human agency are contradictory ideas. Accordingly, a universe where God is completely sovereign and men act as free agents is impossible to reconcile. If God is completely sovereign, human agency is a myth. If men have free will, than God's sovereignty is myth.

According to incompatibilists, the only way to relieve the tension is to limit the sovereignty of God. How else can men make real choices? Some go so far as to deny the absolute sovereignty of God altogether. They argue that God is not in absolute control. This includes control over the choices and actions of men. However, this does not mean things are out of control. As a result of foreknowledge, God is able to predict the outcome of human events. As He does, He responds accordingly, guiding human history to preferred ends. Other incom-patibilists won't go as far as to deny the sovereignty of God. Instead, they argue that God is sovereign, but sets limits on the extent of His sovereignty. Though sovereign, He allows for the free agency of man.

Not surprisingly, those who hold the alternate perspective are known as *compatibilists*. Basically, their view is opposite that of incom-patibilists. Compatibilists also recognize the conflict between sover-eignty and human agency, but uphold both. The essential conflict is left in place. It neither increases the capacity of man, nor diminishes the sovereign power of God. Rather, it allows for both. God's sover-eignty and human agency are equally valid claims. It acknowledges both without seeking to completely reconcile them. The universe that the sovereign God has created includes human agency. God is com-pletely sovereign and there is nothing which is outside of His control or ordaining power. Yet at the same time, human agency is part of His created order without being outside of His control.

> Your faithfulness endures to all generations; you have established the earth, and it stands fast. By your appointment they stand this day, for all things are your servants (Psalm 119:90-91).

> The heart of man plans his way, but the LORD establishes his steps (Proverbs 16:9).

To put it simply (in ways that we cannot understand), God's sovereignty and human agency are not competing ideas, but simply the way God has designed the universe to operate. The fact we cannot reconcile this in our minds does not mean it's not true. How is it that both are possible? Who knows—it's a mystery.

Obviously, if God is sovereign, even our choices are under His rule. But this does not lead to fatalism, as if we are puppets being controlled by hard determinism. Fact is, we do choose. In fact, sometimes we make bad choices and we suffer real consequences from these decisions. We are held responsible for the mistakes we make. There is no sense in any of this that we are being manipulated, or that we are not responsible for the outcomes.

Again, the fact we cannot figure all this out does not mean it's not true. It just means we are not God. To think otherwise is to force God to submit Himself to our rational capacities. This is idolatry.

> You will say to me then, "Why does he still find fault? For who can resist his will?" But who are you, O man, to answer back to God? Will what is molded say to its molder, "Why have you made me like this?" (Romans 9:19-20).

The late James Montgomery Boice, pastor of Tenth Presbyterian Church in Philadelphia, gave an illustration that helped me come to terms with this conflict some years ago. For our purposes in this chapter, I'll offer a similar version of that illustration here. Imagine that the entire known universe is down in a giant hole. It is a hole with sheer walls that cannot be traversed. All of history, time, and humanity exist in the bottom of this hole. Mankind lives down in this hole. Forms nations down in this hole. Marries down in this hole. Has children down in this hole. Works down in this hole. Creates art down in this hole. They even argue about free will down in this hole. They can do anything they set their minds to, except one thing. They cannot get out of the hole. Because of sin, man is not free to remove himself from his condition and deliver himself to God. This is the very point Paul made in the book of Romans on a number of occasions. For example, "all have sinned and fall short of the glory of God, and are justified by his grace as a gift, through the redemption that is in Christ Jesus" (Romans 3:23-24).

If man cannot deliver himself from the peril of his condition before God, someone else has to rescue him from it. By His infinite mercy, God does this very thing in the person of Jesus Christ.

> God so loved the world, that he gave his only Son, that whoever believes in him should not perish but have eternal life. For God did not send his Son into the world to condemn the world, but in order that the world might be saved through him. Whoever believes in him is not condemned, but whoever does not believe is condemned already, because he has not believed in the name of the only Son of God (John 3:16-18).

Let's go back to the beginning for a moment and make one last point. There are some who believe man actually does remove himself out of the hole of his condition. Accordingly, man's will plays an essential role in salvation. These proponents would argue that man indeed has free will as it concerns his salvation. Man is free to choose (or deny) the grace of God in Christ Jesus. Essentially, man's will is not completely affected by sin and retains the capacity (in one way or another) to bring himself to God. Fundamentally, man's will is the primary instrument of his salvation and not the grace of God.

Obviously, there are numerous problems with this perspective, the least of which is not the testimony of Scripture concerning the condition of man. Scripture is replete with an unflattering and brutal description of the will and heart of mankind.

> The heart is deceitful above all things, and desperately sick; who can understand it? (Jeremiah 17:9).

> It is written: "None is righteous, no, not one; no one understands; no one seeks for God. All have turned aside; together they have become worthless; no one does good, not even one" (Romans 3:10-12).

> You were dead in the trespasses and sins in which you once walked, following the course of this world, following the prince of the power of the air, the spirit that is now at work in the sons of disobedience—among whom we all once lived in the passions of our flesh, carrying out the desires of the body and the mind, and were by nature children of wrath, like the rest of mankind. But God, being rich in mercy, because of the great love with which he loved us, even when we were dead in our trespasses, made us alive together with Christ—by grace you have been saved (Ephesians 2:1-6).

Point is, the Bible does not agree with those who would want to leave room for the freedom of the will in man's salvation. This is not to deny the ever-present dilemma that exists in our minds between divine sovereignty and human responsibility. I understand where the need to mitigate the tension comes from, but denying the obvious testimony of Scripture does not relieve anything. It only creates more tension of a different kind.

By proposing free will in salvation, we may think we are defending the essence of the gospel, but we are in fact denying it. Most who hold to free will assume they are preserving the quality of love between Savior and sinner, but they are in fact diluting it. If you add free will to the equation, it actually marginalizes the gospel. The gospel was necessary—exactly and specifically—because man did not have the capacity to bring himself to God. Jesus died because we could not save ourselves in any sense of the word. The gospel is about a rescue mission and not about lending man a helping hand in his search for God.

To state it completely, it was the absence of free will (total depravity) that necessitated the incarnation, death, burial, and resurrection of Jesus Christ. There is no gospel where there is free will. He came into the world to save us principally because we lacked the free will to save ourselves, not because we possessed it. We were "dead in our trespasses." Free will does not assist in defending the gospel; it does away with the need for it.

> The saying is trustworthy and deserving of full acceptance, that Christ Jesus came into the world to save sinners, of whom I am the foremost (1 Timothy 1:15).

"But," some would argue, "what about the necessity to believe? Is not man responsible to have faith? Does he not play some role in his salvation?" The answer is yes. This is true without exception. The necessity of faith is also an undeniable fact substantiated in Scripture.

> If you confess with your mouth that Jesus is Lord and believe in your heart that God raised him from the dead, you will be saved. For with the heart one believes and is justified, and with the mouth one confesses and is saved. For the Scripture says, "Everyone who believes in him will not be put to shame" (Romans 10:9-11).

Many, seeing a contradiction here, balk and choose sides between God and man. If man is unable to respond due to sin, how can he believe? If faith is required but sin makes it impossible for man to believe, how can he be saved? More importantly, how can man be required to do something he is unable to do? These are all valid questions. The Bible does not shy away from them.

> So then he has mercy on whomever he wills, and he hardens whomever he wills. You will say to me then, "Why does he still find fault? For who can resist his will?" But who are you, O man, to answer back to God? Will what is molded

say to its molder, "Why have you made me like this?" Has the potter no right over the clay, to make out of the same lump one vessel for honorable use and another for dishonorable use? (Romans 9:18-21).

Answer? Ultimately, God both causes and supplies the faith that man exercises. Scripture is also clear on this point without any attempt to remove the conflict.

It is God who works in you, both to will and to work for his good pleasure (Philippians 2:13).

God, being rich in mercy, because of the great love with which he loved us, even when we were dead in our trespasses, made us alive together with Christ—by grace you have been saved—and raised us up with him and seated us with him in the heavenly places in Christ Jesus, so that in the coming ages he might show the immeasurable riches of his grace in kindness toward us in Christ Jesus. For by grace you have been saved through faith. And this is not your own doing; it is the gift of God, not a result of works, so that no one may boast. For we are his workmanship, created in Christ Jesus for good works, which God prepared beforehand, that we should walk in them (Ephesians 2:4-10).

As much as we may struggle to understand and make sense of how it is that divine sovereignty and human responsibility co-exist, we must ultimately yield our perspective to that of God's revelation. "But who are you, O man, to answer back to God?"

INSIGHTS FROM THE PAST

But not to insist any longer on the inexplicable abstruseness of this distinction; let what will be supposed concerning the meaning of them that use it, thus much must at least be intended by Arminians when they talk of Indifference as essential to Liberty of Will, if they intend anything, in any respect to their purpose, *viz.* That it is such an Indifference as leaves the will not determined already; but free from actual possession, and vacant of predetermination, so far, that there may be room for the exercise of the self-determining power of the Will; and that the Will's freedom consists in, or depends upon, this vacancy and opportunity that is left for the Will itself to be the determiner of the act that is to be the free act.

And here I would observe in the first place, that to make out this scheme of Liberty, the Indifference must be perfect and absolute; there must be a perfect freedom from all antecedent preponderation or inclination. Because if the Will be already inclined, before it exerts its own sovereign power on itself, then its inclination is not wholly owing to itself: if when two opposites are proposed to the soul for its choice, the proposal does not find the soul wholly in a state of Indifference, then it is not found in a state of Liberty for mere self-determination. The least degree of an antecedent bias must be inconsistent with their notion of Liberty. For so long as prior inclination possesses the Will, and is not removed, the former binds the latter, so that it is utterly impossible that the Will should act otherwise than agreeably to it. Surely the Will cannot act or choose contrary to a remaining prevailing inclination of the Will. To suppose otherwise, would be the same thing as to suppose that the Will is inclined contrary to its present prevailing inclination, or contrary to what it is inclined to. That which the Will prefers, to that, all things considered, it preponderates and inclines. It is equally impossible for the Will to choose contrary to its own remaining and present preponderating inclination, as it is to prefer contrary to its own present preference, or choose contrary to its own present choice. The Will, therefore, so long as it is under the influence of an old preponderating inclination, is not at Liberty for a new free act; of any, that shall now be an act of self-determination. That which is a self-determined free act, must be one which the Will determines in the possession and use of a peculiar sort of Liberty; such as consists in a freedom from every thing, which, if it were there, would make it impossible that the Will, at that time, should be otherwise than that way to which it tends.

Jonathan Edwards, The Freedom of the Will, first published in 1754

4

CHRISTIAN LIBERTY

The Theological Relevance of a Single Malt Scotch

BYRON YAWN

As the story goes, a notable Christian preacher was hosting a dinner for supporters of his radio ministry. It was his way of saying thank you for their generous support over the years. Apparently it's what you do when you have donors.

As everyone sat down at the table, a waitress approached. "May I get you something to drink? Some wine or a cocktail?" A woman in the dinner party spoke up and announced, "Of course not. We are Christians!" She then turned the wine glass at her table setting upside down.

The preacher, without missing a beat, said to the waitress, "In that case, I'll have a scotch."

How brilliant. If Christianity can be reduced to mere nonparticipation in a nonmoral activity, then it's not Christianity at all. If we are to protect the essence of true Christianity (the gospel) from being subsumed by moralism, it's necessary to distance ourselves from these sorts of stereotypes. Strangely, exercising Christian freedom in certain instances may be the only effective defense of biblical Christianity.

This dear Christian lady may be of the opinion that drinking alcohol is unwise for Christians, but what she actually said went much further. The basic point of her diminutive protest was obvious: Anyone who drinks alcohol cannot be considered a Christian. At the least, the implication of her assertion is that committed Christians will not drink. Either way, it's a wrong assertion.

All of this was her opinion and personal conviction on the matter. She is entitled to both. But in this instance, her personal conviction wasn't in line with what Scripture teaches. The Bible allows Christians to consume alcohol. But it does not allow drunkenness. Yet there are those—including entire denominations—who would argue against the Christian's freedom to consume alcohol. Ultimately, their "biblical" defenses cannot stand up to thorough exegesis. And most of the reasonable opponents admit this. Ironically, it is more biblical to choose abstinence with regard to drink when the choice is based on Christian freedom. "I choose not to do drink" is far more biblical than "The Bible says it is wrong."

Christians in America have strong opinions about the place of alcohol in the Christian life. Some say it's wrong, others say it's okay, and there's everything in between. The real question is not whether drink is allowable, but what do you do when people who differ on the matter meet in the church? When it comes to a nonmoral but important issue like alcohol, how should we respond? Where are the limits of Christian freedom? Should we abstain from what the Bible says is allowable simply because others would be offended if we didn't? Does the conscience of another person serve as the authority over mine?

Getting to the "Nonissue"

You know you are facing an issue of Christian liberty when the appropriate answer is both yes and no. And you know you are dealing with it properly when you can take people who are on the opposite sides of a nonessential issue and affirm the convictions of each without contradicting yourself.

"Can I eat meat sacrificed to idols?"

"If it is okay with you, then yes."

"Can I eat meat sacrificed to idols?"

"If it is not okay with you, then no."

As Paul said in Romans 14:22-23:

The faith that you have, keep between yourself and God. Blessed is the one who has no reason to pass judgment on himself for what he approves. But whoever has doubts is condemned if he eats, because the eating is not from faith. For whatever does not proceed from faith is sin.

If you are able to answer yes to both sides of a particular question of liberty, then it demonstrates that the real problem is not whether the given practice is morally acceptable, but the relative consciences of individuals toward that issue. Those individual consciences are influenced by any number of factors—background, culture. The real challenge is upholding the truth on both sides—liberty and conscience. There must be equal diligence. On the one hand, we cannot deny the liberty provided in Christ by allowing a behavior (or activity) to be defined as sinful when it is not. On the other hand, we must uphold sacrificial love by not allowing liberty to exist at the expense of others.

There are always people at the extremes when it comes to matters of Christian liberty. There are those who carelessly flaunt their liberty in the face of others. Liberty for liberty's sake. Their mantra is "You can't tell me this is wrong." Then there are those who choke out all freedom with their personal concerns. Their mantra is "Do as I do." One group rejects anyone controlling them. The other tries to control everyone else. When you can rightly offend the people at both extremes, your stance is probably correct. To be faithful, you cannot yield to either.

The Truth Is in the Middle

The emotions involved in matters of Christian liberty are usually intense. Those opposed to liberty in a particular area can't believe the other side has no problem with it. It's hard for them to see how their consciences don't suffer over such matters. In contrast, those with freedom can't believe the other side has an issue. It's hard for them to see what the problem is. The truth is in the middle. That is where the apostle Paul stood. He was between two perspectives on a rather sticky nonmoral issue in the Corinthian church—that of eating meat sacrificed to idols.

The pagan temples around Corinth, in which the practice of sacrificing meat to various pagan deities was common, functioned as ancient distributors of meat and meat products. They would sell a certain portion of the meat presented in the temple into the marketplace. It was quite possible, then, for a Christian to buy meat not knowing that it had earlier been sacrificed to idols. There were likely instances when a believer knew for certain he was eating meat that had been sacrificed to idols—such as when he ate dinner in an unbeliever's home.

You can see how this had become a major issue in the church. Imagine coming to a barbecue at my home. After you wolf down your burger, I announce, "I bought this meat down at the satanic lodge." It would give you pause. You would immediately wonder whether you had committed some sin before God. Or if I had committed some sin against you. Or you might question the level of my commitment to Christ. Undoubtedly, for this to happen could result in a conflicted conscience. That's how many in Corinth felt. They wanted to know what was right or wrong. Is it okay to eat meat sacrificed to idols? Does it violate the Law of God? Is it wrong? Needless to say, people on both sides of the issue felt very passionate about it.

The idea of meat sacrificed to idols may seem like a strange problem because we don't live in a city with pagan temples on every corner. We're unlikely to encounter it. But the time, place, culture, and era are unimportant when it comes to matters of liberty. We have similar issues in our context; alcohol (as mentioned earlier), dress, entertainment, dancing, and so on. The fundamental conflict Paul was forced to resolve is the same conflict we are forced to resolve anytime we face a matter of Christian liberty in our own context. Whether meat sacrificed to idols, or the appropriateness of drinking alcohol, it always comes down to one basic question: If God does not prohibit it and certain Christians struggle with it, what are we to do? In such scenarios, who is right? Whose choice prevails? How do we handle nonessential issues while avoiding the potential for offense on both sides?

Cutting the "Baby" in Two

Remember when King Solomon proposed cutting a disputed baby in half? His approach exposed the truth about who the real mother was. In a similar way, Paul's gospel-saturated logic here cuts the baby in half and gets to the root of the issue. It protects the gospel and the individual. It upholds freedom and encourages restraint without denying the need for either. Only the cross can do that. Without the cross, the exercise of liberty ends in the abuse of others or it ends in the bondage of a few. Here are the principles Paul used to find balance on the issue.

Principle #1

Never Turn a "Both/And" into an "Either/Or" Simply to Satisfy Moralists

Paul did not alter his conviction, adjust his behavior, or create a law where none existed simply to satisfy those who struggled with a behavior God did not prohibit. To state that positively: Paul allowed the implication of gospel liberty to roam free. He did not use qualifiers to salve the consciences of some. He did not cage Christian liberty simply because some are uncomfortable standing near it. This is what he wrote to those who struggled:

> Therefore concerning the eating of things sacrificed to idols, we know that there is no such thing as an idol in the world, and that there is no God but one. For even if there are so-called gods whether in heaven or on earth, as indeed there are many gods and many lords, yet for us there is but one God, the Father, from whom are all things and we exist for Him; and one Lord, Jesus Christ, by whom are all things, and we exist through Him (1 Corinthians 8:4-6 NASB).

Those who were opposed to eating meat sacrificed to idols saw it as a compromise of Christian standards and morals. They felt it un-Christian and something committed Christians did not do. To them, eating meat sacrificed to idols was a sign of spiritual decline. It was unquestionably wrong. But they could not point to any Scripture to justify their convictions—which is usually the case in such matters. It was a matter of how they felt based on their experience, tradition, or culture, and not what the Bible said. At the least, in their minds, it was a better option not to participate. Fact is, they had no biblical justification for their position.

On the other hand, the meat eaters—who had no struggle over this at all—did have biblical and theological grounds to justify their participation. To them, eating meat offered to idols was a nonissue and they could prove it. Ironically, it was those who had no problem with the "socially unacceptable" practice who were in the right. Their argument was watertight and founded on Scripture:

> We know that there is no such thing as an idol in the world, and that there is no God but one...yet for us there is but one God, the Father, from whom are all things, and we exist for Him (verses 4,6 NASB).

This was the theological and biblical justification being offered by those who were okay with the practice. This would have been something they said. Paul was quoting back to them their theological basis for their liberty. It's a solid reason. Not just any truth, mind you. They picked the cornerstone of Christian theism, the most fundamental theological statement available to Christianity: There is only one God. That is the foundation of all other theological thought. Monotheism made eating meat—even that sacrificed to idols—okay.

Here's the logic: "There is but one God" means there are no others. Logically, then, idols are meaningless. Therefore, meat is not actually sacrificed to a god when it is offered to an idol. Therefore, there is nothing wrong with eating meat sacrificed to idols. Even meat sacrificed to idols is inherently good and nonmoral. Ultimately, it is okay to eat. "You cannot tell me it is wrong." Theologically, those who held this view were correct.

Christ Has Set Me Free

If that weren't enough, the people on the liberty side of this issue tagged on a Christological basis for their freedom: "...and one Lord, Jesus Christ, by whom are all things, and we exist through Him" (verse 6 NASB).

Whatever they are before God they are because of Christ. Not because of anything they had or hadn't done. They were touching on realities central to the gospel. The concepts of substitution and justification were prevalent in their reasoning. Paul elaborated on this elsewhere in great detail—such as in Galatians 2:16:

> …nevertheless knowing that a man is not justified by the works of the Law but through faith in Christ Jesus, even we have believed in Christ Jesus, that we may be justified by faith in Christ, and not by the works of the Law; since by the works of the Law shall no flesh be justified (NASB).

When you put the two thoughts together the implications are obvious. Theologically, it's a nonissue. Eating meat sacrificed to idols in and of itself was not a sin. Meat is not inherently sinful. The Bible does not forbid it.

Yes, Christian liberty can be abused. Yes, there are contexts that may lead to sin. Yes, there is the need for a discerning application of liberty, but there is no need to view it as sin, or repent of it. Eating meat sacrificed to idols was allowable. The believers in Corinth had the freedom to do this and enjoy it. There was nothing about eating meat sacrificed to idols that affected their standing before God. "Bon appetit," said Paul.

The Qualification That Never Comes

What you expect Paul to do here is qualify his statement by saying, "But it's safer to take the high ground and just avoid eating such meat altogether. If for nothing else, do it for appearance's sake. You can eat meat, but I wouldn't." This is what some Christians do. They say, "It's okay, but I have chosen not to do it because not doing it is a better option." But Paul didn't say anything about a better option. He only said there is freedom.

No doubt there were people who wanted Paul to qualify his words. They were not comfortable with what Paul was saying. In some ways, it would have been easier if Paul had said the opposite—that eating such meat was wrong, period. Then he could have avoided the conflict altogether. But Paul never does that. Paul would never deny the truth no matter which group he was around. He never said something was wrong when God had not declared it wrong. He had spent a lifetime doing that as a Pharisee; he wasn't going to start doing that now.

In fact, there were moments when Paul intentionally ignored the preferences of some—the legalists—simply because they viewed their preferences as an essential part of the gospel. It was here that Paul pressed liberty in order to reinforce the truth. He knew exactly when this was needed. He allowed Timothy to be circumcised so as to not cause an unnecessary offense to those hearing the gospel (Acts 16:3). On the other hand, he refused to allow Titus to be circumcised before those who held circumcision as essential (Galatians 2:3). This is why Paul's tone is different in Galatians and Colossians than it is in Romans and 1 Corinthians. In the former, the essence of the gospel was at stake. In the latter, it was not.

What's notable is that Paul was not simply conceding the point made by those who said it was okay to eat meat sacrificed to idols. Paul wholeheartedly agreed with their basic conviction. He affirmed it. So not only did he refuse to say what the nonmeat eaters might want him to say; he went out of his way to affirm the convictions of the meat eaters. Paul was in disagreement with anyone who wanted to "legitimize" their argument by taking the high ground of moralism on this issue.

> "All things are lawful," but not all things are helpful. "All things are lawful," but not all things build up (1 Corinthians 10:23).

> Eat whatever is sold in the meat market without raising any question on the ground of conscience. For the earth is the Lord's, and the fullness thereof (1 Corinthians 10:25-26).

> I know and am persuaded in the Lord Jesus that nothing is unclean in itself, but it is unclean for anyone who thinks it unclean (Romans 14:14).

It's telling that Paul did not fall into a trap on either side of this issue—reckless liberty on the one side, or prudish legalism on the other. He kept the truth out of the ditch. Which is where you want to end up.

Paul had the gospel in his sights at all times. He knew where this balance came from. He took his cues from Jesus Himself.

> Do not think that I have come to abolish the Law or the Prophets; I have not come to abolish them but to fulfill them. For truly I say to you, until heaven and earth pass away, not an iota, not a dot, will pass away from the Law until all is accomplished. Therefore whoever relaxes one of the least of these commandments and so teaches others to do the same will be called least in the kingdom of heaven, but whoever does them and teaches them will be called great in the kingdom of heaven. For I tell you, unless your righteousness exceeds that of the scribes and Pharisees, you will never enter the kingdom of heaven (Matthew 5:17-20).

We end in imbalance and cause division anytime we turn a both/and into an either/or. We either rob people of their liberty, or we minimize people's convictions. Doing either never ends well. The gospel leads us to balance by calling us to the cross in our experience and attitude with others.

We Have the Total Freedom to Restrict Our Freedom

Just because we can justify our freedom biblically does not mean that we are absolutely free to live in any way we want—even within those behaviors or actions God has allowed. This is the other side of the argument. Anyone who defends freedom for freedom's sake is just as guilty of forgetting the gospel as the legalist. The moralist makes the mistake by trying to control others; the latter make the mistake of forgetting others.

There are limitations to our freedom—even on the things that God permits. But it's not morals, or preference, or another's conscience (in the way we typically understand it) that controls the limits of our freedom. Nor should it be. That would be a denial of the gospel. Rather, it is the liberty to set aside our liberty for others. *Love* is the greatest liberty we have.

Principle #2

On Preference Issues,
Call People to Die to Self and Not Conform to You

Despite the fact that I am free of all men, I am still the servant of all men. That truth which trumps even my freedom in Christ is not the conscience of another or preference of others, it is freedom from self. The freedom to die to self and serve others. Love is the limit of my freedom where freedom is allowed. Love for others has the jurisdiction to restrict my theologically and biblically substantiated freedom, even for those who are on the other side of an issue. That's Paul's point in 1 Corinthians 8:7: "However, not all possess this knowledge. But some, through former association with idols, eat food as really offered to an idol, and their conscience, being weak, is defiled." Not everyone is in the same place spiritually and has the same knowledge when it comes to eating meat sacrificed to idols.

A desire to serve the faith of our brother in Christ is what creates a balance in our choices. The libertine sees no problem with any choice. The legalist sees only their choice. The weaker believer sees only one choice. The mature believer sees two and is able to choose either.

If Paul did not say what the moralists wanted him to say in 1 Corinthians 8:4-6, in verse 7 he said what the libertines wished he had never said: "Love people." There were many who did struggle with meat sacrificed to idols in a very specific way. They were saved out of paganism and had participated in meat sacrificed to idols on a regular basis. It was part of their past. It presented a particular temptation. It was very possible for them to be dragged back into paganism by the careless exercise of someone's liberty in this area. For this person, the restriction of liberty was essential and right.

The issue here is not whether a given action or behavior is right or wrong in and of itself, but whether it is prudent in every situation. The whole idea of love for the individual should make us reconsider some things. As Paul said, "'All things are lawful,' but not all things are helpful. 'All things are lawful,' but not all things build up. Let no one seek his own good, but the good of his neighbor" (1 Corinthians 10:23-24).

If we selfishly cherish our freedom—freedom for freedom's sake—we violate a different principle. To selfishly run over others is just as wrong as requiring something of someone that God does not require. It is the opposite mistake. There is something greater to consider—other people. This is what Paul is getting at when he says, "However not all men have this knowledge." That is, not everyone is where we are. It's reasonable to assume that if someone had not made these theological premises their own, they would have doubts about the appropriateness of eating meat sacrificed to idols. If the implication of the gospel has not sunk in, you will struggle with various nonissues. Especially if, in your previous life, you were involved in those nonissues in a manner that was actually immoral.

What if you had a hard time getting over the idea that meat sacrificed to idols actually assuaged a pagan deity? Given the context of paganism and idol worship and the role sacrifices played, it's reasonable to assume that anyone who had been involved in that would have a hard time disassociating meat from an inherently evil practice. It would be a struggle for many.

In this instance, it does not matter whether a behavior is actually wrong or not. It would be wrong for *them*. Their former way of life was still part of their consciousness. They had been forgiven of it, but had not yet fully realized the practicality of this statement. They were free objectively, but not free practically.

This type of thing happens all the time in churches. Here in Nashville, musicians who come to us from a career in music struggle to disassociate their career as a performer from their place as a worshipper. This can conflict with their service in church. Some are reluctant to use their gifts until they get their head right. This makes sense. I can tell them there's nothing inherently wrong with using their talents in church, but it would be foolish of me to force it. It's better if I wait on them.

Or what if you were of the opinion that it was okay for Christians to consume alcohol, but you had a brother in your midst who was saved out of alcoholism? Would you drink in front of that person? Only if you were inconsiderate and intent on exercising your freedom at any cost. Of course you would limit your freedom. To do otherwise would be un-Christian.

This was the very situation unfolding in Corinth. Many of the new believers could not approach meat objectively. They knew the facts about their freedom in Christ, but they had not gotten comfortable with them yet: "Some, through former association with idols, eat food as really offered to an idol, and their conscience, being weak, is defiled" (1 Corinthians 8:7).

Apparently they had tried to make it work, but it was still too difficult for them. It caused them to stumble. They could not do it. To them it was sin. Paul described these brethren as those who have weak consciences.

Paul wasn't demeaning them when he said that. He means something very specific. He actually has compassion for them. The conscience is that faculty which discerns right from wrong in the human soul. It's that part of us which makes a moral judgment. It's the red light–green light aspect of our decision-making ability. Basically a weak conscience, as described in this text, is one that cannot handle liberty in a certain area. For these people to exercise their freedom to participate in meat sacrificed to idols would be a disaster for them. They had not broken free from their previous experience and could disassociate from their previous sin.

If we fail to live cautiously before such people, we could inadvertently lead them to sin against their conscience. That's because they have not yet come to a place where they can biblically assess an issue and make an informed decision as to what to do with it. They are not okay with certain things despite the fact they have every objective reason to be okay with them.

A conscience may not allow some people to be comfortable with something that they are free to do. These people have not yet bridged the gap between the realities in the gospel and their participation in nonissues. They experience a real conflict with the thought of doing certain things they are actually at liberty to do.

Our Response to *This* Person

In addressing the Corinthians, Paul was quick to restate the theological basis for liberty when it came to eating meat that had been sacrificed to idols. He wanted to reassure them that he was not saying they had to adopt the convictions of another person on an issue that God has not prohibited. Just to make sure they understood he is not making a law where one does not exist, Paul said, "Food will not commend us to God. We are no worse off if we do not eat it, and no better off if we do" (1 Corinthians 8:8). In every way this was a nonessential. The issue was a matter of love.

By the language Paul used, we see that the problem of meat sacrificed to idols was not a trivial thing. Not to a person who struggled with it. In the next few verses he uses some dramatic language: "stumbling block," "ruined," "sinning against," "wounding," "sin against Christ." This is a person, due to previous experiences, who cannot handle the matter of eating meat. For this person, the others were to be careful with their liberty so as not to injure his conscience or drag him into sin:

> Take care that this liberty of yours does not somehow become a stumbling block to the weak. For if someone sees you, who have knowledge, dining in an idol's temple, will not his conscience, if he is weak, be strengthened to eat things sacrificed to idols? For through your knowledge he who is weak is ruined, the brother for whose sake Christ died. And so, by sinning against the brethren and wounding their conscience when it is weak, you sin against Christ. Therefore, if food causes my brother to stumble, I will never eat meat again, that I will not cause my brother to stumble (1 Corinthians 8:9-13).

The exhortation that Paul gives is one of caution. By a careless use of our liberty a person could be pressed to do something he is not prepared to do. Apparently some believers in the church were taking their liberty right up to the edge and pressuring those who could not handle the liberty to approve and even participate in it. This was unloving. In a strange way, those who cherished freedom had become moralists themselves by forcing others to conform to their position.

There were times when Paul had to defend the Christian's freedom from moralism. And there were other times he had to defend people's weak consciences from the thoughtless exercise of freedom. There were times when Paul would order meat. And there were other times he would order vegetables. This is the latter.

The Cross Makes Our Sacrifice Make Sense

Perhaps your journey has been similar to mine. You have trekked out of legalism and are now living in the freedom of the gospel of Jesus Christ. You are the ex-smoker. Almost every restriction of freedom you consider an attack on grace. Your heart is in the right place, but your gun is aimed at the wrong people.

Far greater than the power of freedom in nonmoral issues is the freedom we have to sacrifice our rights for others. The greatest liberty we have been given is from the tyranny of self. If you do not see this, then you have not truly understood the extent of the gospel.

How do you get freedom-loving Christians to restrict their rights for others? By pointing them to the cross of Christ: "…the brother for whose sake Christ died." When it comes to matters of preference, we do not call people to conform to us, but to the cross. That answer is correct 100 percent of the time.

Basically, in 1 Corinthians 8, Paul steps in front of the Corinthians' cavalier display of liberty for the sake of the "weaker brother." The apostle calls for those who are "free" to put on a servant's heart towards those who don't possess the same freedom. What would convince the proud Corinthians to deny themselves a freedom simply because someone else does not possess the same freedom? Answer: the cross of Jesus Christ. The cross makes our self-sacrifice on any issue make perfect sense.

INSIGHTS FROM THE PAST

That I may open then an easier way for the ignorant—for these alone I am trying to serve—I first lay down two propositions, concerning spiritual liberty and servitude:

> A Christian man is the most free lord of all, and subject to none; a Christian man is the most dutiful servant of all, and subject to every one.

Although these statements appear contradictory, yet, when they are found to agree together, they will do excellently for my purpose. They are both the statements of Paul himself, who says, "Though I be free from all men, yet have I made myself a servant unto all" (I Cor. ix. 19), and "Owe no man anything but to love one another" (Rom. xiii. 8). Now love is by its own nature dutiful and obedient to the beloved object. Thus even Christ, though Lord of all things, was yet made of a woman; made under the law; at once free and a servant; at once in the form of God and in the form of a servant...

There are very many persons who, when they hear of this liberty of faith, straightway turn it into an occasion of license. They think that everything is now lawful for them, and do not choose to show themselves free men and Christians in any other way than by their contempt and reprehension of ceremonies, of traditions, of human laws; as if they were Christians merely because they refuse to fast on stated days, or eat flesh when others fast, or omit the customary prayers; scoffing at the precepts of men, but utterly passing over all the rest that belongs to the Christian religion. On the other hand, they are most pertinaciously resisted by those who strive after salvation solely by their observance of and reverence for ceremonies, as they would be saved merely because they fast on stated days, or abstain from flesh, or make formal prayers; talking loudly of the precepts of the church and of the Fathers, and not caring a straw about those things which belong to our genuine faith. Both these parties are plainly culpable, in that, while they neglect matters which are of weight and necessary for salvation, they contend noisily about such as are without weight and not necessary.

How much more rightly does the Apostle Paul teach us to walk in the middle path, condemning either extreme and saying, "Let not him that eateth despise him that eateth not; and let not him which eateth not judge him that eateth" (Rom. xiv. 3)! You see here how the Apostle blames those who, not from religious feeling, but in mere contempt, neglect and rail at ceremonial observances, and teaches them not to despise, since this "knowledge puffeth up." Again, he teaches the pertinacious upholders of these things not to judge their opponents. For neither party observes towards the other that charity which edifieth. In this matter we must listen to Scripture, which teaches us to turn aside neither to the right hand nor to the left, but to follow those right precepts of the Lord which rejoice the heart. For just as a man is not righteous merely because he serves and is devoted to works and ceremonial rites, so neither will he be accounted righteous merely because he neglects and despises them.

Martin Luther, "On Christian Freedom," 1520

HELL

Grim, But Not a Fairy Tale[1]

MIKE ABENDROTH

My first job had nothing to do with fast food or newspapers. It involved dressing up like a werewolf. It was not a paid job, but I had many responsibilities. I was hired to yell, growl, moan, and snarl. Tall teens were especially desirable for my particular job. I was a live "prop" inside a haunted house. Well, to my knowledge, it was not actually haunted. It was an old vacant house transformed every year into a spooky haunt. Customers would pay hard-earned money to navigate their way through it. The proceeds went to charity. So I worked to scare people for a nonprofit endeavor.

The 30 of us who worked in this haunted house would put on our makeup during the one hour prior to "show time." In my case, teased hair (I had a lot of locks in 1975), gallons of hairspray, base coat facial cream, and cool glow-in-the-dark fangs were on the menu. Just before the doors were opened to let people into the eerie mansion, we would scatter and hide throughout the house. I was tasked with knowing every nook and cranny of the place so that I could roam anywhere I wanted and pounce on unwitting prey.

To me, scaring the wits out of people is one of the simple pleasures in life, which is why I did not care about making any money from that job. I enjoyed volunteering my time to startle grown men and women.

Jolting juveniles was also addicting. I am not sure why it is so fun, but I still enjoy scaring my kids today.

Speaking of the reflex action of fear, some of the people visiting the haunted house were so frightened that they would just fall down on the floor with the rapidity of a tire iron sinking to the bottom of a swimming pool. But not all the petrified patrons were so entertaining. Some spit on my face, and others tried to sock my cosmetic-laden face with a right jab. A couple of those fists ended up connecting.

Many such haunted houses boast of the fact that all who enter will have nightmares after they exit. In some cases I have seen these houses promoted as "Hell Houses." But I have never liked seeing Halloween haunts associated with hell, which is real. No matter how frightening a spooky house might be, it is still a joy ride compared to the real and eternal horrors of hell. Words cannot express the gulf of difference there is between the two.

Why This Chapter?

Interestingly, more unbelievers acknowledge an actual hell than they concede Jesus as the only Savior. What explains such prevalent belief in an eternal judgment? Is it because the justice of God is imprinted on every human heart on account of the fact men and women are image bearers of God Himself? Every person born has an internal desire for wrongs to be made right. No one enjoys seeing a murderer walk free without paying his or her debt to society. But here is the rub: The unbeliever's notion of hell is nothing like the biblical definition of eternal punishment. The unbeliever's version of hell is more akin to a Halloween house. If you read any survey, from Barna to Gallup, about Americans' belief in hell, you will notice that a majority of them believe in hell. But that number of "believers" would turn into a miniscule minority if the people polled actually understood what the Bible teaches about hell.

Consider some of the initial thoughts that go through the heart and mind of a new Christian. The neophyte believer revels in forgiveness, praises the work of Jesus Christ, and desires to get to know God better through the Bible. The Damocles-like sword of God's ultimate justice and punishment no longer burdens this person. The reality of hell, which used to be like a 500-pound weight on the person's chest, is now, by grace, wonderfully removed. Hallelujah! The new believer rejoices for himself or herself, knowing that the prospect of going to hell is gone due to Christ's perfect atonement. The resurrection has confirmed Christ's finished work on behalf of the sinner. But then another thought begins to creep into the soul. The prospect of hell still crowds itself into the mind of the redeemed saint, but this time out of concern for loved ones, and not self.

The Christian swallows hard because she apprehends the doom of every one of her unregenerate family members and friends. The terror of terror is amplified as the new Christian learns more about the Bible's description of hell. No longer informed by the world's distorted conception of hell, the Christian reads the Bible and is instantly struck by the severity of hell, as defined by Scripture. In every case, the Word of God is much scarier than the fanciful human portrayals of hell, even if some are, like Dante's inferno, close to the biblical characterization.

Said another way, when people first become Christians—when they are born again—hell takes on more foreboding overtones. Newly converted Christians, due to the Holy Spirit's illumination of Holy Writ, come to read and believe in the Bible with a newly found comprehension. While they might not understand everything they read in the Bible, they know it is true because the Spirit bears witness to its validity and truth. Hell is therefore a very sure and petrifying proposition. The more you read the Bible and believe it, the scarier hell becomes.

It is for this reason that new Christians, if not thinking properly, might even be tempted to refuse to believe eternal punishment exists, essentially inserting an index finger into each ear while humming loudly, desperately trying to mute the volume of Scripture's teaching on eternal judgment. After all, hell is incredibly scary! Yet hell is supposed to scare people. A lot. As unbelievers, they wrote off hell's population as made up of really evil people like Hitler, Stalin, and their ilk. But then the believer realizes that even "good" non-Christians like their loved ones are sinners, and that every sinner is destined for hell, they become alarmed. Hell is for *every* sinner—not just the worst.

This chapter attempts to demonstrate that hell is scary—and that the reality of hell *must* be believed. We will examine five reasons hell is bloodcurdling. Leaning not on tradition, fiction, myths, or fables, let's look toward the Bible as our only instructor about hell. Ralph Powell's guidance is wise:

> It must always be remembered that the Bible is our rule of faith for the doctrine of hell, however difficult the doctrine may seem for natural reason or for human sentiment. Scripture leaves no doubt about the terrible nature and the eternal duration of hell. Rejection or neglect of this doctrine will have dire effects upon the true health and mission of the church. [2]

1. Hell Is Bone-Chilling Because Jesus Taught It Was True

I am always amused when someone says, "I like the words of Jesus, but not Paul." Stated naively and ignorantly, such words speak volumes about the person's knowledge of Scripture. Somehow they think Jesus is all love (He is loving, but He is so much more) and that Paul preached only judgment. There is no more loving person in the universe than Jesus Christ, yet He regularly affirmed and taught the doctrine of endless punishment.

Do you ever wonder why there are some theologians who are evangelical in every area of the faith yet deny the eternality of hell? Simple answer: Unless one continually bows to the revelation of the Bible, hell is too horrible to be believed. I regularly tell people, "The only reason I believe in the horrors of hell is because they are clearly taught in the Bible, especially by the Lord Jesus Christ."

Jesus was not the only one who taught people about a literal hell; the beloved John taught the doctrine of hell (Revelation 20:15), Paul the apostle instructed churches about eternal punishment (2 Thessalonians 1:9), and Peter affirmed hell (2 Peter 2:4). But by far, "the strongest support of the doctrine of Endless Punishment is the teaching of Christ, the Redeemer of man." [3]

Listen to the words of Jesus Christ and note carefully the different ways hell is described—and these details are just from the Gospel of Matthew:

> I say to you that everyone who is angry with his brother will be liable to judgment; whoever insults his brother will be liable to the council; and whoever says, "You fool!" will be liable to the hell of fire (Matthew 5:22).

> If your right eye causes you to sin, tear it out and throw it away. For it is better that you lose one of your members than that your whole body be thrown into hell. And if your right hand causes you to sin, cut it off and throw it away. For it is better that you lose one of your members than that your whole body go into hell (Matthew 5:29-30).

> I tell you, many will come from east and west and recline at table with Abraham, Isaac, and Jacob in the kingdom of heaven, while the sons of the kingdom will be thrown into the outer darkness. In that place there will be weeping and gnashing of teeth (Matthew 8:11-12).

> Do not fear those who kill the body but cannot kill the soul. Rather fear him who can destroy both soul and body in hell (Matthew 10:28).

> Just as the weeds are gathered and burned with fire, so will it be at the end of the age. The Son of Man will send his angels, and they will gather out of his kingdom all causes of sin and all law-breakers, and throw them into the fiery furnace. In that place there will be weeping and gnashing of teeth (Matthew 13:40-42).

> So it will be at the end of the age. The angels will come out and separate the evil from the righteous and throw them into the fiery furnace. In that place there will be weeping and gnashing of teeth (Matthew 13:49-50).

> If your hand or your foot causes you to sin, cut it off and throw it away. It is better for you to enter life crippled or lame than with two hands or two feet to be thrown into the

eternal fire. And if your eye causes you to sin, tear it out and throw it away. It is better for you to enter life with one eye than with two eyes to be thrown into the hell of fire (Matthew 18:8-9).

The king said to the attendants, "Bind him hand and foot and cast him into the outer darkness. In that place there will be weeping and gnashing of teeth" (Matthew 22:13).

Woe to you, scribes and Pharisees, hypocrites! For you travel across sea and land to make a single proselyte, and when he becomes a proselyte, you make him twice as much a child of hell as yourselves (Matthew 23:15).

You serpents, you brood of vipers, how are you to escape being sentenced to hell? (Matthew 23:33).

Cast the worthless servant into the outer darkness. In that place there will be weeping and gnashing of teeth (Matthew 25:30).

Then he will say to those on his left, "Depart from me, you cursed, into the eternal fire prepared for the devil and his angels. For I was hungry and you gave me no food, I was thirsty and you gave me no drink, I was a stranger and you did not welcome me, naked and you did not clothe me, sick and in prison and you did not visit me." Then they also will answer, saying, "Lord, when did we see you hungry or thirsty or a stranger or naked or sick or in prison, and did not minister to you?" Then he will answer them, saying, "Truly, I say to you, as you did not do it to one of the least of these, you did not do it to me." And these will go away into eternal punishment, but the righteous into eternal life (Matthew 25:41-46).

If you are a Christ follower, you must believe what Jesus explicitly taught—and He certainly taught about a future place of punishment! Since Jesus the Creator taught about hell more than anyone else, His credibility is the ultimate object of the retractors' scorn. Outspoken atheist Bertrand Russell proudly crowed, "I do not myself feel that any person who is really profoundly human can believe in everlasting punishment…I must say that I think all this doctrine, that hellfire is a punishment for sin, is a doctrine of cruelty." [4] Ultimately, arguments against the Creator prove futile. What did Jesus say?

Christian, read your Bible regularly. When you do, you will immediately recognize the voice of your Shepherd confirming your notions of hell as a real doctrine. More than that, you will see how integral the reality of hell is, especially in the teaching of the Lord Jesus. If the incarnation of love Himself taught that hell was authentic, you had better believe hell is an actual place, and you had better believe it is scary.

2. Hell Is Scary Because God Is in Hell and God Is Scary

The philosopher Jean-Paul Sartre is said to have proclaimed, "Hell is people." What makes hell "hell"? Most believe God to be absent in hell. Is that true? How does God's omnipresence factor into this matter of hell? Read Revelation 14:9-11 as you ponder the question, Is God in hell, at least in some capacity?

> Another angel, a third, followed them, saying with a loud voice, "If anyone worships the beast and its image and receives a mark on his forehead or on his hand, he also will drink the wine of God's wrath, poured full strength into the cup of his anger, and he will be tormented with fire and sulfur in the presence of the holy angels and *in the presence of the Lamb*. And the smoke of their torment goes up forever and ever, and they have no rest, day or night, these worshipers of the beast and its image, and whoever receives the mark of its name."

The context describes the doom of Babylon and her followers. God's undiluted wrath is poured forever and ever upon those who worshipped the beast. And the text states that the Lamb, Jesus Christ, will be there. In what way is God in hell? God is in hell as punisher. No more will unbelievers receive God's common mercy, kindness, and goodness. In hell, long gone are the God-given pleasures of marriage, food, and sunshine. God casts away His favor and love and is personally in hell as the righteous Judge.

Paul does not contradict John when he states, "They will suffer the punishment of eternal destruction, *away from the presence of the Lord and from the glory of his might*" (2 Thessalonians 1:9). How are Revelation 14 and 2 Thessalonians 1 reconciled? Answer: Both are true, yet each teaches a different aspect of the same truth. Sinners in hell are barred from the grace of Jesus Christ, but fully experience His wrath and holy justice. Jonathan Edwards agreed, saying, "God will be the hell of the one and the heaven of the other." [5] In heaven, Jesus Christ will function as Advocate and Mediator, while in hell, Jesus, the omnipresent God, will operate as Tormenter, Judge, and Eternal Executioner.

While some Bible passages teach God as personal avenger ("It is a fearful thing to fall into the hands of the living God"—Hebrews 10:31), at the same time, God can declare to impenitent sinners,

> Not everyone who says to me, "Lord, Lord," will enter the kingdom of heaven, but the one who does the will of my Father who is in heaven. On that day many will say to me, "Lord, Lord, did we not prophesy in your name, and cast out demons in your name, and do many mighty works in your name?" And then will I declare to them, "I never knew you; depart from me, you workers of lawlessness" (Matthew 7:21-23).

God's goodness is never given to unbelievers in hell. Instead, His holy wrath is poured out upon them. The bottom line is that God rules in hell. Satan does not reign there; rather, he is punished along with all other rebels. God is the Judge, Jury, and Executioner of the divine court. When people talk about "partying with their buddies" in hell, they are vainly trying to pacify their consciences and assuage their minds from pondering the grim realities of hell.

3. Hell Is Spine-Chilling Because People Deserve Their Punishment

Not one person in hell deserves to be in heaven. Every inhabitant will have earned a place there. God can never compromise His holy justice;

therefore, He can never negotiate with sin. Every sinner has offended God and His Son, which means every sinner will be punished to the full extent of the law of God. John Blanchard positively extracts some hope from this truth: "There is therefore a sense in which hell is good news. It not only shows that in the final analysis God can never compromise with sin, but it puts an end to the possibility of sin ever again breaking out and ruining His creation."[6] But terrifyingly, because God can never compromise with sin, every sin will certainly be punished and every unforgiven human will not escape that awful day of judgment.

John Calvin knew the ramifications of insulting God: "Even if there were no hell, I would still shudder at offending him alone."[7] The King of kings has been offended by the sin of rebels. But God is more than simply offended; His law has been broken and justice must take place. Hell is where vindication takes place. Every sin is infinitely horrible because it has been committed against an infinitely holy God. Jonathan Edwards recognized unbelievers deserved their just sentence because they offended God and His laws:

> The glory of God is the greatest good; it is that which is the chief end of creation; it is of greater importance than anything else. But this is one way wherein God will glorify Himself, as in the eternal destruction of ungodly men He will glorify His justice. Therein He will appear as a just governor of the world. The vindictive justice of God will appear strict, exact, awful, and terrible, and therefore glorious.[8]

The only hope is for sinners to cry out to the God of justice, who thankfully is a gracious Savior as well.

4. Hell Is Frightening Because It Is Eternal

Some teachers attempt to restrict hell's eternality. Others, in vain, espouse doctrines about purgatory to assuage the consciences of people or to extract money from them. Is hell really eternal? Does it truly last forever? Listen to Jesus describe hell, and note what He says about its duration:

If your hand causes you to sin, cut it off. It is better for you to enter life crippled than with two hands to go to hell, to the *unquenchable fire*. And if your foot causes you to sin, cut it off. It is better for you to enter life lame than with two feet to be thrown into hell. And if your eye causes you to sin, tear it out. It is better for you to enter the kingdom of God with one eye than with two eyes to be thrown into hell, *"where their worm does not die and the fire is not quenched"* (Mark 9:43-48).

To the extent that heaven is eternal life, so too must hell be eternal. Jesus uses the exact same word for "eternal" in the following sentence, "These will go away into *eternal* punishment, but the righteous into *eternal* life" (Matthew 25:46). The glory for believers is that heaven is eternal—in other words, heaven never ends. Sadly, for unforgiven sinners, the torments of the damned shall never cease. As God is eternal, so too is the punishment for every treasonous sinner. Scary. It is said of John Drexel that he asked his readers to think of a million to the tenth power number of years, and then to think of this period of time as a second of time in hell.[9]

I remember breaking my foot during a basketball game and needing to have surgery to correct the injury. I knew that in a few short days, the surgeons would fix my problem and I would soon be on the mend. I received hope from this assurance. Hope is an essential part of life, especially in tough times. But there is no hope in hell, no relief, and maybe worst of all, no hope of relief. Read what Jonathan Edwards, Charles Spurgeon, and Christopher Love said as they tried to help their readers to understand eternity:

Nor will they ever be able to find anything to relieve them in hell. They will never find any resting place there; any secret corner, which will be cooler than the rest, where they may have a little respite, a small abatement of the extremity of their torment. They never will be able to find any cooling stream or fountain, in any part of that world of torment; no, nor so much as a drop of water to cool their tongues.

They will find no company to give them any comfort, or do them the least good. They will find no place, where they can remain, and rest, and take breath for one minute: for they will be tormented with fire and brimstone; and they will have no rest day nor night forever and ever. [10]

In hell there is no hope. They have not even the hope of dying—the hope of being annihilated. They are forever—forever—forever lost! On every chain in hell, there is written "forever." In the fires there, blaze out the words, "forever." Above their heads, they read, "forever." Their eyes are galled and their hearts are pained with the thought that it is "forever." Oh, if I could tell you tonight that hell would one day be burned out, and that those who were lost might be saved, there would be a jubilee in hell at the very thought of it. But it cannot be—it is "forever" they are cast into the outer darkness. [11]

Suppose all the mountains of the earth were mountains of sand, and many more mountains still added thereto, till they reached up to heaven, and a little bird should once in every thousand years take one (grain of) sand of this mountain, there would be an innumerable company of years pass over before that mass of sand would be consumed and taken away, and yet this time would have an end; and it would be happy for man, if hell were no longer than this time; but this is man's misery in hell, he shall be in no more hope of coming out after he hath been there millions of years, than he was when he was first cast in there; for his torments shall be to eternity, without end, because the God that damns him is eternal. [12]

Hell does not reform people. Hell is punitive. Hell yields an infinite amount of punishment for a temporal sin because that temporal sin is against an infinitely holy God. This concept is not foreign to the modern reader. For example, although murder only takes a few seconds to accomplish, the punishment of the murderer can yield 40 or more years of imprisonment. The greater the crime is, the greater the punishment must be. How horrendous is any treasonous sin against the Creator? God's justice will prove just. And awful.

5. Hell Is, and Will Be, Petrifying Because There Are Degrees of Punishment in Hell

Hell will be excruciating for everyone who goes there, but the Bible teaches that it will be worse for some than for others. It will be bad for all, but worse for some. There is severe punishment for all in hell, but even more severe for some people. Scripture says,

> How much worse punishment, do you think, will be deserved by the one who has trampled underfoot the Son of God, and has profaned the blood of the covenant by which he was sanctified, and has outraged the Spirit of grace? (Hebrews 10:29).

> And you, Capernaum, will you be exalted to heaven? You will be brought down to Hades. For if the mighty works done in you had been done in Sodom, it would have remained until this day. But I tell you that it will be more tolerable on the day of judgment for the land of Sodom than for you (Matthew 11:23-24).

How can there be gradations of punishment in hell? What is the basis for some people's hell being "hotter" than others? Listen to the apostle John:

> I saw the dead, great and small, standing before the throne, and books were opened. Then another book was opened, which is the book of life. And the dead were judged by what was written in the books, according to what they had done (Revelation 20:12).

Sinners are judged in hell by "what they had done." Contrary to the erroneous teaching that people are in hell only because they have rejected Jesus Christ (which is a very heinous sin indeed, but every sin is grotesque when you remember the One who has been sinned against), people will be in hell for rejecting Christ *and* for every other sin they have committed. In other words, every transgression a person commits earns a greater degree of torture in hell. Hell is also worse for those who squandered their knowledge of God and their opportunities (like regularly hearing the gospel and having access to the Word of God). Since every sin must be punished, it is not hard to mentally grasp that those who have sinned more (like Stalin) will suffer more and those whose sins are fewer will suffer less. Jonathan Edwards commented on the degrees of eternal punishment, saying, "The longer sinners live, the more wrath they accumulate." Why? Because of the aggregation of sin. For the criminal on earth, it would be better for him to get caught earlier than later. Prison awaits him either way, but the sentence will be less if he has committed fewer crimes. The same holds true for hell and its denizens.

Read John Blanchard, Thomas Watson, and Jonathan Edwards, and let the full shock wave of truth hit you:

> If a sinner is to remain unconverted, the sooner he dies the better, otherwise every further sin he commits will make things that much worse for him in eternity. [13]

> The coolest part of hell is hot enough, but there are some who shall have a hotter place in hell than others. All shall go into that fiery prison, but some sinners God will thrust into the dungeon. [14]

> Sinners in hell would give anything to turn the clock back and have committed even one sin less. [15]

Now What?

First, if you have been saved by the grace of the Lord Jesus Christ alone, through faith alone in Him, you ought to be eternally and abundantly joyful. I was having a bad day recently but I stopped my pity party with the reminder that because of Jesus Christ and His substitutionary death on my behalf, I don't have to endure eternal punishment in hell. Furthermore, I am allowed to dwell in the house of the

Lord forever. I honestly felt much better when I recalled those truths, and you should too each time you reflect on your status before God.

What thankfulness should flood the heart of every believer, knowing that Jesus assuaged the wrath of God that he or she deserved! At Calvary, during those three dark hours of judgment, God the Father poured out His fury upon His Son, the sinless Savior. Christ's sacrificial death amounted to Him experiencing the eternal torments of an eternity in hell, except those terrors were condensed into three hours. No wonder Christ prayed the way He did in the Garden of Gethsemane. Be glad that the Son obeyed the Father and you are the recipient of God's love for rebels. Rejoice that God the Father raised Jesus from the dead, thus confirming His acceptance of Christ Jesus' great atonement.

Second, knowing what you have been saved from, go and tell everyone who will listen about the free grace of God for those who trust in Christ Jesus and His life, death, and resurrection. Tell your family about repentance, righteousness, and the judgment to come. Preach the gospel of grace to them. Plead. Beg. Pray. Be an ambassador of the gospel like Paul was (2 Corinthians 5:20-21).

The good news about working at a haunted house for fun was that I could leave anytime I chose. I was in charge. I was not forced to be a resident. The props were made with fake blood and most of them needed electricity in order for their eyes to light up or to make their heads swirl and scream. Haunted houses are but dim reflections of the kind of horror people will face in hell. About the only thing both have in common is that both are meant to be ghastly, with only one truly horrifying its inhabitants.

If you happen to be reading this book and you have yet to trust in Christ Jesus as Lord and Savior, I want you to be traumatized toward a proper response to the veracity of hell as depicted by Joseph Alleine:

> Oh, better were it for you to die in a jail, in a ditch, in a dungeon, than to die in your sins. If death, as it will take away all your comforts, would take away all your sins too, it were some mitigation; but your sins will follow you when your friends leave you, and all your worldly enjoyments

shake hands with you. Your sins will not die with you as
a prisoner's other debts will; but they will go to judgment
with you there to be your accusers; and they will go to hell
with you there to be your tormentors. [16]

The bow of God's wrath is bent, and the arrow made ready on the
string, and justice bends the arrow at your heart, and strains the bow,
and it is nothing but the mere pleasure of God, and that of an angry
God, without any promise or obligation at all, that keeps the arrow
one moment from being made drunk with your blood. Thus all you
that never passed under a great change of heart, by the mighty power of
the Spirit of God upon your souls; all you that were never born again,
and made new creatures, and raised from being dead in sin, to a state
of new, and before altogether unexperienced light and life, are in the
hands of an angry God. However you may have reformed your life
in many things, and may have had religious affections, and may keep
up a form of religion in your families and closets, and in the house of
God, it is nothing but his mere pleasure that keeps you from being this
moment swallowed up in everlasting destruction. However uncon-
vinced you may now be of the truth of what you hear, by and by you
will be fully convinced of it. Those that are gone from being in the like
circumstances with you, see that it was so with them; for destruction
came suddenly upon most of them; when they expected nothing of it,
and while they were saying, Peace and safety: now they see, that those
things on which they depended for peace and safety, were nothing but
thin air and empty shadows.

The God that holds you over the pit of hell, much as one holds a
spider, or some loathsome insect over the fire, abhors you, and is dread-
fully provoked: his wrath towards you burns like fire; he looks upon
you as worthy of nothing else, but to be cast into the fire; he is of purer
eyes than to bear to have you in his sight; you are ten thousand times
more abominable in his eyes, than the most hateful venomous serpent

is in ours. You have offended him infinitely more than ever a stubborn rebel did his prince; and yet it is nothing but his hand that holds you from falling into the fire every moment. It is to be ascribed to nothing else, that you did not go to hell the last night; that you was suffered to awake again in this world, after you closed your eyes to sleep. And there is no other reason to be given, why you have not dropped into hell since you arose in the morning, but that God's hand has held you up. There is no other reason to be given why you have not gone to hell... Yea, there is nothing else that is to be given as a reason why you do not this very moment drop down into hell.

O sinner! Consider the fearful danger you are in: it is a great furnace of wrath, a wide and bottomless pit, full of the fire of wrath, that you are held over in the hand of that God, whose wrath is provoked and incensed as much against you, as against many of the damned in hell. You hang by a slender thread, with the flames of divine wrath flashing about it, and ready every moment to singe it, and burn it asunder; and you have no interest in any Mediator, and nothing to lay hold of to save yourself, nothing to keep off the flames of wrath, nothing of your own, nothing that you ever have done, nothing that you can do, to induce God to spare you one moment.

Jonathan Edwards, "Sinners in the Hands of an Angry God,"
first preached in Enfield, Connecticut, July 8, 1741

DEMONS

Spiritual Swashbuckling

CLINT ARCHER

It was a dark night. Raining. I awoke to frantic knocking on my cabin door. Youth camps often come with various genres of drama, from relationship angst to teary confession sessions. As a camp counselor, I had encountered a diverse array of spiritual emergencies on my watch, ranging from the need to rebuke a bevy of mean girls to confiscating contraband magazines from the guys' dorm. But the look in this kid's eyes was one of genuine terror. Something was wrong. I grabbed my Bible and charged through the pouring rain in pursuit of the young man who had been sent to summon me. When I got to the dorm room, all 12 teenage boys were standing outside, shivering wet.

They sheepishly confessed that they had been experimenting with an occult game, glassy-glassy. This is where people supposedly channel spirits, which move a glass over a lettered board to eerily spell out instructions from the netherworld. The boys breathlessly recounted what they had witnessed. Shortly after they had turned out the lights and sealed the door, they heard an intense crying sound in the room like that of a baby who had been pinched. This was followed by hissing noises and more high-pitched cries. The stunned boys all looked thoroughly traumatized. This was no prank being played on the camp counselor. I wanted to ask which one of them was disturbed enough to bring satanic paraphernalia to a Christian camp, and why none of the others were man enough to put a stop to it. Instead, I clutched my Bible, boldly kicked open the door, and flipped on the light switch.

After a halting flicker, the room was flooded with a fluorescent blaze, and I immediately saw the creature. It was as hideous as any I had seen before. Wild eyes glaring at me, sharp fangs bared, curved claws gripping a shredded down pillow, it was perched as if spring-loaded to pounce at my jugular. This was the most terrified cat I had ever encountered.

The poor animal's back leg had been clipped between the metal bed frame and the wall, probably when one of the camp's dumbest dozen shifted the cot during their would-be foray into the spirit realm. I moved the bed with my foot and the beast made a limping beeline for the door. The boys' fear turned to throbbing embarrassment. Without a word I trudged back to my cabin, rolling my eyes in disdain, and shaking uncontrollably from the adrenaline and cold.

As I lay on my hard mattress with the lights on, I kept wondering why my first reaction had been to expect that the encounter would be with a demon. I had honestly thought that a satanic specter was a legitimate explanation for the fear that gripped those young men. What sane person hears, "There's a noise in my dorm room," and concludes, "This could be a demon"? It bugged me that I had reacted so superstitiously. But I realized that what had sparked my fear was the unknown. I knew almost nothing about glassy-glassy, the occult, or the demonic realm. I knew that the Bible declared demons to be real. And I had heard stories of demonic manifestations from people who had heard it from people who probably read about them on the Internet. But I was clueless as to what the Bible said about demons beyond the fact that they existed.

I decided then that I would learn more by ferreting out every verse in the Bible alluding to spiritual warfare and demonic activity. If the spirit dimension was real and demons were still at large today, I wanted to be well informed of their operations. And if all the demons mentioned in the Bible were now in some sort of hibernation mode, I wanted to be biblically certain of that.

My feline foundling had provided me with a vivid metaphor:

Flipping on a light switch was all it took to strip a situation of futile phobias that are bred in the darkness of ignorance. I needed scriptural illumination to dispel my spiritual naïveté.

There Are No Experts

In my studies on spiritual warfare, one illusion I was summarily disabused of was the notion that there are experts in the field. Any reading you do on the subject soon demonstrates that the pundits cite experience as their primary source of information, and those experiences vary greatly. Either the expert has assimilated an anthology of anecdotes as related by other people, or just as commonly, he or she claims to have personally witnessed some sort of manifestation.[1]

One such individual's experience has led him to make some conclusions of his own that are unsubstantiated—for example, "It is my observation that no more than 15% of the evangelical Christian community is completely free from Satan's bondage."[2] He makes other authoritative assertions of this sort: "Demonic influence is not an external force in the physical realm; it is the internal manipulation of the central nervous system."[3] And he even suggests sins of omission and commission can be blamed on demonic control over believers: "Anything bad which you cannot stop doing, or anything good which you cannot make yourself do, could be an area of demonic control."[4]

There are a few problems with the limited information available on demons. The usual suspects in the lineup are subjective interpretations, unverifiable claims, and of course, the big E on the eye chart: the untrustworthiness of the source.

The Flimsy Sword of Subjective Interpretation

Subjective interpretations plague the research. Some of the information comes from people who swear they "felt a presence" of evil, or their hair stood on end when they walked into a room. Like a flimsy sword, this type of claim makes some noise, but is useless to serious study. God has not equipped humans with a sixth sense to be brandished like a Geiger counter to detect invisible spirits. Our subjective feelings are a flimsy sword in the battle of truth.

The Rusty Blade of Unverifiable Claims

You can't trust a rusty blade in a duel, and you can't rely on fanciful, unverifiable claims when formulating a doctrine. Supernatural experiences are by definition exempt from the standards of inquiry in the natural sciences. This pops open a portal to outrageous abuses. Anyone looking for attention can claim a paranormal experience. This can be any variety of ghost hunter, from your well-intentioned, slightly delusional weirdo to an outright liar who is craving attention from his pew buddies at church.

This phenomenon is not limited to the church. Reports of supernatural activity such as alien kidnappings come from all corners of secular society as well. Demonology is simply the church's flavor of a wider cultural obsession with the supernatural—an obsession confirmed by the popularity of television shows and specials featuring vampires, angels, and psychics.

But the most undermining issue with experience-based information in the field of demons is the untrustworthiness of the source.

Liars Make Unreliable Sources

I'm not saying that demonic activity never happens. Rather, I'm merely pointing out that the reports of such activity can't be trusted as authoritative. Think about it: Demons are a genus of beings known for being masters of deception (John 8:44). Who would choose to base their research on what these lying liars say? It seems to me that general issue equipment for demon hunters should not be holy water, but rather a pinch of salt.

In his book *Demon Possession and the Christian*, Fred Dickason recounts an interview he said took place with a spirit: "I queried the demon regarding his undercover mind control. He admitted to controlling the brain through electrical and chemical changes. 'We have power in that,' was his confession. Again we do not take this as scientific evidence, but his confirmation of controlling the mind through the brain, must be considered. Why would he give away such damaging information except he were under pressure from the Lord?"[5]

Why indeed? Perhaps so that he can deceive his quarry into making statements that detract Christians from the truth? That's just my guess, but I'm no expert. Then again, neither is anyone else. There are no experts in this field. No one person has any more *reliable* information than anyone else.

So where does that leave us? If we want to know about demons, is there anywhere we can turn for trustworthy information that runs no risk of the contamination of error and deception? Enter the Word of God.

The Sword of the Spirit

One trustworthy supernatural source of information is the Holy Spirit, who inspired the writings of Scripture, "for the word of God is living and active, sharper than any two-edged sword" (Hebrews 4:12). A belief in the doctrine of inerrancy is the only safeguard against the chronic confusion that obscures this topic. The apostle Paul told Timothy that "all Scripture is breathed out by God and profitable for teaching, for reproof, for correction, and for training in righteousness, that the man of God may be complete, equipped for every good work" (2 Timothy 3:16-17). The apostle Peter gave us the assurance that we as Christians have "been given all things pertaining to life and godliness" (2 Peter 1:3).

If God wanted to tell us what to do and how to do it, He is certainly capable of it. He is not suffering from a speech impediment. God can and has revealed everything we need to live a life pleasing to Him, including how to deal with the spiritual realm. As long as we rightly interpret the Bible, we will have the light of knowledge guarding us from the fear and confusion that comes from speculation and ignorance.

There is one interpretive principle that is most helpful to keep in your hermeneutic tool belt: that of recognizing the difference between *descriptive* accounts and *prescriptive* instructions.

Description Is Not Prescription

This principle is important to keep in mind as you read about demons being cast out as you go through the four Gospels and the book of Acts. These books are historical narrative accounts of events that occurred. What we learn from them is that demons exist, that they can possess unbelievers, and that they were able to be cast out by Jesus and the apostles, who had His authority to do so. But these *descriptive* accounts are not intended to be a manual *prescribing* any how-tos for Christians today.

The New Testament epistles are crammed with prescriptive instructions on how Christians are to live, behave, and think. It is very significant to note that none of these epistles give any instruction whatsoever on how to (or even whether to) cast out a demon. In a book written by God for His people to let them know what to do and how to live, the fact that there is absolutely no instruction on how to cast out a demon is a lesson in itself.

Demons, we learn from the biblical descriptions of their abilities and proclivities, are extremely dangerous. One account we have in Acts would almost be humorous if it were not so chilling. In Acts 19 we are told, "Some of the itinerant Jewish exorcists undertook to invoke the name of the Lord Jesus over those who had evil spirits, saying, 'I adjure you by the Jesus whom Paul proclaims'" (verse 13). Apparently these guys had witnessed Paul casting out demons. And taking that description as a prescription on how to do the same, they confronted a demon-possessed man. The result? "But the evil spirit answered them, 'Jesus I know, and Paul I recognize, but who are you?' And the man in whom was the evil spirit leaped on them, mastered all of them and overpowered them, so that they fled out of that house naked and wounded" (verses 15-16). Yikes. I facetiously wrote in the margin of my Bible, "i.e., don't try this at home."

Lesson learned: Just because someone else has his or her license to operate heavy machinery does not mean you have the right or ability to drive a forklift. We do not apply descriptions of Moses parting the Red Sea directly, so why assume Paul's authority over demons is ours for the wielding? This can be dangerous—just ask the itinerant Jewish exorcists in Acts 19.

Parry Error with Truth

The Bible supplies us with helpful information concerning the spirit world. Demons are spirit beings who are fallen angels, cast out of heaven and operating in this world to oppose the rule of God on earth (Revelation 12:9). We can assume that they are immortal, intelligent, and consummately evil. And as Satan's minions, they are never ever to be trusted as a source of any information (John 8:44).

Demons can, like Satan, orchestrate temptations (Luke 4:13), infiltrate society through teachings (1 Timothy 4:1; James 3:15), instigate false religions (1 Corinthians 10:20), hinder the ministry of believers (2 Corinthians 12:7), possess unbelievers (though with some challenges involved in finding a suitable host as in Luke 11:24), tell fortunes (Acts 16:16), and empower convincing fake miracles (2 Thessalonians 2:9; Revelation 16:14).

However, demons cannot do whatever they want. They are limited to operating within parameters set by God, like when Jesus granted the 72 evangelists "demonic immunity" (Luke 10:19). Demons cannot possess believers (1 John 5:18), nor can they control a believer's mind, or make a believer sin (James 1:14). But they may somehow also be able to influence the mind to be tempted to sin, probably through external teachings and situations (Acts 5:3).

There is no evidence in Scripture that visible demonic activity should be expected as a normative part of the Christian life, despite the many occurrences in the Gospels. As Alex W. Konya points out,

> It should be recalled that historically most cases of demon possession described in the New Testament occurred in idolatrous or occultic settings such as Galilee, Phoenicia or Ephesus. It seems reasonable to conclude from this that demon possession is most likely to be encountered in persons whose past involves serious involvement with the occult or idolatry. [6]

I'm not saying that demons are in a low-power, screensaver mode today. They are active in variegated ways, but they can function in subtle and sophisticated ways too. In societies where the supernatural is accepted wholesale as a given, the reports of overt demonic activity tend to be more prevalent. Shamanism, animism, ecstatic ritualism, and urban-brew Satanism are fertile soil for demonization. Reports abound from missionaries who witness Amazon tribal rituals or encounter African witch doctors carrying out ancestral worship. Some pastors in the South Pacific islands report sustained demonic activity—where the paranormal intersects with the normal—as a matter of routine.

On the other hand, in societies where an acknowledgment of genuine supernatural events is generally held in condescending disdain, demonic activity is far more subtle and covert. The rationalism of Westerners is easy to use against us to keep us duped. The supernatural is relegated to the world of fanciful fiction, the likes of that found in TV shows and vampire novels. There are few Western secularists who would entertain the notion that demons are real. The supernatural is viewed as mythical, unscientific, and therefore primitive. But the danger of such naïve denial is as insidious as the alternative.

C.S. Lewis warned in his *Screwtape Letters*, "There are two equal and opposite errors into which our race can fall about devils: one is to disbelieve in their existence. The other is to believe and feel an excessive and unhealthy interest in them."[7]

The face of evil may look less like a tormented cat than you think; it may be the clean-cut cult leader or the esteemed seminary professor who is propagating godless arguments that fortify the strongholds of demonic influence in society and the church. This threat should not be ignored. It is as devastating to impressionable minds as demon possession is to a body.

Our Riposte: A Right Response

Despite the conspicuous absence of instruction on how to engage the enemy forces around us, the New Testament is replete with marching orders for Christians. Our Commander-in-Chief has not left us to guess His will, or to devise a strategy apart from His guidance. He has instructed us on what to do and how to do it. Not surprisingly, there are no recipes for holy water or scripts for incantations. Instead, there are commands to apply the lessons of Scripture and trust God to do the rest.

First we are told to combat demonic influence with spiritual virtue, not in the physical realm (2 Corinthians 10:4-5; Ephesians 6:11-18). Our task is to resist temptation by submitting to God's will (James 4:7).

If you feel tempted to try to bind or rebuke a demon, just bear in mind that God has specifically told His people to refrain from confronting demons in this way (2 Peter 2:11; Jude 9-10). Where did we get the idea it was acceptable to talk to demons or address Satan in our prayers? Not from Scripture. I've heard pastors, frustrated by a malfunctioning church sound system, derail their prayer to God with phrases like, "And now we bind you Satan in the name of Jesus, you are not welcome here, and we resist your presence, and we shun your distractions." For one thing, Satan is not omnipresent or omniscient. My guess is he is probably occupied with activities more important than attacking an overhead projector or snapping a worship leader's guitar string. But even if demons were active in a church building, there is no biblical evidence to suggest that the influence would include mysterious gremlin-type interference of our physical apparatus. And even if it did, that is no license to talk to the demon.

The overarching principle in our response to the demonic realm is to understand that there are spiritual schemes at play (2 Corinthians 2:11) and that we do not wrestle against flesh and blood (Ephesians 6:11-12), so the resistance needs to be spiritual, not physical. There is no protective spell or vial of holy water that works as well as simply walking in God's will, obeying Him, being a worshipper of Christ, evangelizing the lost, and praying to God about any fear or situation that occurs.

When the apostle Paul preached the gospel in the hip, metropolitan neighborhood of Ephesus, the effects were dramatic. After the scandalous whipping of the itinerant Jewish would-be ghost-busters, the city of Ephesus was ablaze with change:

And this became known to all the residents of Ephesus,

both Jews and Greeks. And fear fell upon them all, and the name of the Lord Jesus was extolled. Also many of those who were now believers came, confessing and divulging their practices. And a number of those who had practiced magic arts brought their books together and burned them in the sight of all. And they counted the value of them and found it came to fifty thousand pieces of silver. So the word of the Lord continued to increase and prevail mightily (Acts 19:17-20).

That is a lot of esoteric kindling. Ephesus must have been a demonic stronghold. That the converts from pagan magic burned books to the value of 50,000 pieces of silver is remarkable. One can imagine just how prolific the magic arts must have been in that city. The instructions God gave the fledgling church in Ephesus contain a conspicuous absence of physical methods or techniques for resisting demons. Instead, Paul speaks about the armor of God, which is described as virtues to be spiritually donned by all believers:

> Put on the whole armor of God, that you may be able to stand against the schemes of the devil. For we do not wrestle against flesh and blood, but against the rulers, against the authorities, against the cosmic powers over this present darkness, against the spiritual forces of evil in the heavenly places. Therefore take up the whole armor of God, that you may be able to withstand in the evil day, and having done all, to stand firm. Stand therefore, having fastened on the belt of truth, and having put on the breastplate of righteousness, and, as shoes for your feet, having put on the readiness given by the gospel of peace. In all circumstances take up the shield of faith, with which you can extinguish all the flaming darts of the evil one; and take the helmet of salvation, and the sword of the Spirit, which is the word of God, praying at all times in the Spirit, with all prayer and supplication. To that end keep alert with all perseverance, making supplication for all the saints, and also for me, that words may be given to me in opening my mouth

boldly to proclaim the mystery of the gospel, for which I
am an ambassador in chains, that I may declare it boldly,
as I ought to speak (Ephesians 6:11-20).

This is the most direct and detailed instruction in the whole Bible
on how believers are to treat the demonic realm. There isn't a single
hint of casting out, binding, or in any way engaging demons or their
possessed hosts. That is either a blundering oversight of eternal pro-
portions, or the most compelling evidence that Christians are not supposed to engage the spiritual world directly.

Resisting the Urge to Be a Swashbuckler

In my teenage years I fenced competitively and I fancied myself
quite the swaggering swashbuckler. I was indomitable in my age group
(as I remember it), but I'll never forget what it was like to draw swords
against the national champion. He practiced at my club, so on occasion
I challenged him to a duel. My goal was to score a single point. Fenc-
ing him was an exercise in humility. Even when he was going easy on
me, I could barely register where the blade was at any given moment.
Once I got hit squarely on the back. How he bent his blade to reach
my spine while still standing before me was an embarrassing enigma.
I was clearly outclassed.

Lessons like that lingered with me into my pastoral career. There are
times when I hear of pastors challenging demons by castigating them
or invoking formulas to bind them, drive them out, or in some other
way wrangle compliance from them. I shudder at the thought of draw-
ing spiritual swords with a creature as powerful as a demon.

The doctrine of spiritual warfare is a scary one for many Christians,
and with good reason. When we are blindfolded by misinformation,
we really have no idea what we are getting into. But as soon as we aim
the biblical floodlight of truth on the matter, we are comforted to know
that our God is invincible, and He is on our side. Rather than become
fascinated by the intrigue of the spiritual world, we should focus on
the accessible truth in our laps, the Scriptures. In them is everything we
need to keep us safe and help us to live godly lives. All of our spiritual

swashbuckling should be directed at the enemy within our reach: sin's temptations, demonic teachings, and the residual enemy within our own flesh. Demons are out of our league, and we should praise God that He doesn't expect us to draw swords with them. He is our shield, our defender, and our fortress. "What then shall we say to these things? If God is for us, who can be against us?" (Romans 8:31).

INSIGHTS FROM THE PAST

And though this world, with devils filled,
should threaten to undo us,
we will not fear, for God hath willed
his truth to triumph through us.
The Prince of Darkness grim,
we tremble not for him;
his rage we can endure,
for lo, his doom is sure;
one little word shall fell him.

Martin Luther's hymn, "A Mighty Fortress Is Our God," circa 1529

PROVIDENCE, CONCURRENCE, AND THE MIRACULOUS

When God Hacks into Life

CLINT ARCHER

Computers have stealthily infiltrated the fabric of human society like a genial tribe of cannibals moving into the neighborhood. Prophetic doomsday filmmakers play on the unnerving suspicions we all have that one day these indentured electronic appliances could rise up against us. And I'm not talking about a malicious microwave overheating your pasta out of petty spite. The world's most lethal military arsenals are run by what is essentially a video game console. Our banks, our public transport systems, our family pictures, our medical histories, and our social networks are all enmeshed in a digital matrix. As a society, we have cavalierly handed over our most intimate details and most valuable assets to an inanimate hive of electrons with the simple trust that a machine will do what it is told to.

And thankfully, that is mostly true. Even when a CPU crashes in a silent hara-kiri protest, we simply reboot with our backup drive and all our dearly departed data are resurrected. We take comfort in knowing that sinister, self-aware artificial intelligence is the stuff of science fiction. Computers only do what humans tell them to. But isn't that just as scary? The harrowing truth is that the electronic puppet strings that govern every level of our existence can be plucked and pulled by anyone with the expertise, equipment, and desire to become a hacker.

Hackers comprise a subculture of computer users who are not content to use software the way it was designed. Their desire is to master the programmable intricacies of a system in order to intrude and manipulate or destroy information. Profit, protest, or simple glee may fuel a hacker's subterfuge; but the result is always that an unwanted user gains access to that which is intended to be guarded.

The hacking underworld has spawned a variety of breeds. The so-called "white hat" hackers are benevolent programming experts who use their abilities to discover security weaknesses for the purpose of rectifying the vulnerability. But the variety of hacker that triggers chills down the spines of network administrators, bank managers, stock analysts, and army generals the world over is the notorious "black hat" hacker. As the archetypal name suggests, this species is compelled by nefarious goals—for example, political anarchy, ethical protest, personal blackmail, or simple pilfering. Black hat hackers are anti-establishment predators who come out in the twilight, like vampires, and employ their special powers to prey on the rest of us.

Now imagine you discovered there was a person who could hack into the matrix of life and manipulate even the most inviolable laws of nature. This person could, say, reverse scientific laws, crash the economy, bring a powerful kingdom to its knees, cure the incurable, explain the inscrutable, multiply foodstuff for the hungry, bring the dead back to life, and generally manipulate anything and everything we think we understand. How would you respond?

It Is God's Prerogative to Hack into Life

Most of us prefer order, structure, and predictable laws to govern our world. As much as gravity hinders the enjoyment of moving furniture, we are grateful for its predictability and consistency when we go for a walk. What scares us is when an immutable law ends up out of our control and it is suddenly in the control of someone else. We don't mind that we cannot leap tall buildings in a single bound, as long as no one else can either. If a select group of the population were superhuman, we would suddenly feel handicapped and vulnerable. Anything supernatural or paranormal is frightening because it lies outside our realm of expertise. It leaves the most reliable laws of nature temporarily unreliable—like knowing there is a hacker out there who knows the password to your bank account. It can be disconcerting.

When educated individuals read the Scriptures and discover the pages are sprinkled liberally with events that could never be explained by natural laws, they are understandably skeptical. If there is a being that can hack into the matrix of nature, society, medicine, economics, or any other sphere we like to control, that leaves us with a sense of vulnerability and uncertainty. But the Bible paints God's uninhibited involvement and control in our lives as a doctrine to be cherished, not feared.

Jesus offered comfort to the anxious with an injunction to remember how the Father feeds inconsequential, winged vermin like ravens (Luke 12:24). I love how, in Jesus' worldview, God is intimately and minutely involved in His creation. Ravens survive because God actively feeds them. In Hebrews 1:3 we are told that Jesus "upholds the universe by the word of his power." In Matthew 10:29 we are assured that not even the cheapest culinary commodity, a sparrow, dies without the explicit say-so of the Father. God did not design a self-contained software system, hit the enter button, and step back like a detached digital watchmaker to watch the program run. His attention is constantly engaged with His creation even to the minutest detail.

Understandably, the knowledge that this is the case can be a bit bewildering for some. Even King David punctuated Psalm 139, which extols God's omniscience, with the reeling admission, "This boggles my mind" (vernacular for verse 6):

> O LORD, you have searched me and known me! You
> know when I sit down and when I rise up; you discern my
> thoughts from afar. You search out my path and my lying
> down and are acquainted with all my ways. Even before
> a word is on my tongue, behold, O LORD, you know it

altogether. You hem me in, behind and before, and lay your
hand upon me. Such knowledge is too wonderful for me;
it is high; I cannot attain it (Psalm 139:1-6).

And we can understand why. Our independence recoils at the thought
of being so closely scrutinized. But the knowledge of God's involvement in and attention to our lives is intended to be a comfort, not a
curse.

Let us never forget exactly whose creation this is. God is God, after
all, and one of the great job perks of being God is that there are no
limits placed on control. Omnipotence is a handy utensil when you
want something done, as when a nation needs to win a battle before
sunset (Joshua 10:12-13), or new eyes need to be plugged into a blind
man with the ease of assembling a Mr. Potato Head (John 9:6-7). God
made the world for His own glory and enjoyment, and He reserves the
right to run it any way He chooses. Psalm 135:6 states this categori-
cally, "Whatever the LORD pleases, he does, in heaven and on earth, in
the seas and all deeps." And Psalm 115:3 says, "Our God is in the heavens; he does all that he pleases."

God's Tools for Hacking into the Matrix of Life

Computer hackers use tools to circumvent the security of a system. These tools include social engineering (soliciting passwords from
people in the company), rootkits, viruses, worms, and many other
delightful-sounding contraptions used to pick the privacy lock of a
program.

God also uses various implements to hack into our lives. His toolbox has three main compartments in it—namely, miracles, providence,
and concurrence. Each of these has a place and purpose in the way God
involves Himself in our lives. Let's start with the flashiest, albeit the rar-
est of the tools: miracles.

Miracles

As appropriate as it is to designate it as such on a Hallmark congrat-
ulatory card, the birth of a baby is not, strictly speaking, a miracle. Nor
is it theologically accurate to modestly declare, "It's a miracle I passed

that exam with so little time to study." I commend the impulse to give God glory for His involvement in the natural processes of your life, but for the sake of theological precision, let's define a miracle more conservatively. A miracle is when God *breaks the laws* of nature to accomplish His will by doing that which is scientifically impossible.

Examples abound in Scripture: causing a heavy metal axe head to float in the water to save a destitute person from going into debt (2 Kings 6:5-7), morphing H_2O into fine wine to spare a host embarrassment (John 2:7-10), or parting a sea to keep His people safe from pursuant Egyptian hordes (Exodus 14:21-23). Jesus displayed His deity by effortlessly performing an array of miracles in every conceivable realm: geographically (calming the storm with a word), medically (generating the growth of a withered hand), creatively (feeding 5000 with two fish), chemically (water transubstantiated into wine), and spiritually (casting out tenacious demons cohabiting a human's body), and even in thanatology (resurrecting the deceased). Jesus wielded absolute control over disease, demons, death, and nature.

The reason Jesus performed those deeds was to prove something about His claims. When a person declares confidently that he is God, either we smile and nod, or we institutionalize him. But if he can cause a corpse to sit up in its coffin, we do well to pay attention. In order to have the clout that was intended, the miracles Jesus performed had to be undeniable, irrefutable, verifiable, instant, complete, and downright impossible. If a deed could be faked, it would not accomplish its purpose of distinguishing the miracle worker as one sent from God (John 9:30-32).

The same can be said for the apostles, who proliferated a spectacular sampling of miracles during the infant years of the church. That is precisely why those activities were called signs and wonders (Acts 2:43; Hebrews 2:4) and "the signs of a true apostle" (2 Corinthians 12:12). They were signposts that pointed to a truth God was underscoring.

Miracles have a specialized function in God's dealing with humanity—namely, to prove something. God was either proving a point (e.g., I am God—see Exodus 3 and the burning bush), or He was authenticating a spokesman (see Exodus 7 and the serpentine rod), or He was providing protection to prove His involvement in the lives of His people (see Exodus 14 and the parted Red Sea).

Though miracles do not occur on such a grand scale anymore, nor are they specifically linked to individuals with a gift of miracles, there is no biblical reason to believe that God cannot or does not perform miracles today. I would merely caution that before appending the coveted label of *bona fide* miracle, we pause to compare the candidate to the standard of a true, Bible-grade miracle. We simply can't put Miracle Whip cream or the "miraculous results" of teeth-whitening products on par with the law-busting impossibilities of genuine signs and wonders.

There is another tool that God uses to affect the world, which though less obvious to the casual observer, is no less astonishing when perceived rightly. I'm referring to the mind-boggling tool of providence.

Providence

The compartment in God's toolbox that supplies Him with His most used instrument is that of providence. Whereas a miracle is an example of God's involvement in His creation by *breaking* the laws of nature, providence refers to God's operation *within* those laws to accomplish His will.

One punchy example is found in Matthew 17:24-27. The persnickety collectors of the two-drachma temple tax pounced on Peter with an inquiry as to whether or not Jesus paid for the upkeep of the temple in Jerusalem (though this encounter happened in Capernaum). Ordained rabbis were exempt from this tax, but it seems these collectors were gloating about Jesus' lack of formal recognition.

Jesus made the point to Peter that He was exempt from this tax, not only as a rabbi but because He is the Son of God, the temple is technically His temple! However, to avoid offending the tax collectors' sensibilities, Jesus instructed Peter to go withdraw some cash in a most unusual manner. Jesus told him to pull a fish out the sea, knowing that the creature would be bearing a shekel coin in its mouth. The shekel was worth four drachma, meaning it would cover the annoying toll for both Peter and Jesus.

Now just ponder for a moment what went into supplying the

precise amount of money needed at the perfect moment in time to meet this specific fiscal need. First, some unwitting accomplice to the provision would have had to irrecoverably drop a coin into the seawater. Then an unsuspecting fish would instantaneously be attracted to that falling object and would scoop the currency into its mouth. The cash-bearing cavity needed to be roomy enough to ensconce a coin, but not so large as to facilitate swallowing said coin. The fish, not yet having its appetite satisfied, would be attracted to whatever bait Peter tossed in the shallow waters of the Galilean beach, and would get ensnared in the fisherman's hook, only to be relieved of both man-made metallic burdens by a bemused Peter, who would now be in possession of the exact change needed to cover his tax and his Lord's. It is not hard to see why people think of this as a miracle. It is a remarkable example of God's involvement in the everyday affairs of people, and yet at no time was a law of nature violated. The entire event could, by an unbelieving observer, be termed uncanny coincidence.

This demonstrates the difference between miracles and providence. Miracles require a supernatural explanation; no other will suffice. Providence can be explained entirely by natural means, but the believing eye sees the invisible maneuvering of creation to order and ordain those means.

The fishy shekel is a particularly conspicuous example of God's interference. But there are times that God's involvement is no less real but far less perceptible. For example, did you thank God for the rent or house payment money this month? Unless you were expecting an eviction notice and had a last-minute reprieve by some unexpected income, you probably didn't notice God's tender provision through a complex stream of events that converged in you having enough money to pay your rent. The family you were born into, the school you attended, the grades you got, the education you obtained, the job interview you secured, the impression you gave, and the job you received are all links in a chain that God forged to provide for you this month.

Just because the workings of God flow beneath your awareness does not mean they aren't there. When sound reaches your ears in church, you might not see the sound crew working the desk, the wire cables in the ceiling, or the vibrating airwaves carrying the information to you, but those conduits are all in place for your benefit, whether you are aware and thankful for them or not. Providence is the way God runs His creation moment by moment. When you open your eyes to this fact, you see just how involved He is.

Bible verses about sparrows falling to the ground begin to make more sense. Confidence in God's protection becomes less mysterious. Trust in God's provision becomes less challenging. And obedience to His commission to evangelize is less daunting. All of life is minutely ordered and incessantly propelled by the hand of God.

When bad things happen, our confidence can be unshakeable. We who love God know that "all things work together for good, for those who are called according to his purpose" (Romans 8:28). "All things" includes natural disasters like earthquakes and tsunamis, man-made problems like recession and kitchen fires and flat tires, and even the sinful decisions people make like murder and slander. God monitors all these events and activities and decisions in the matrix of life, and He is able to constantly make adjustments and provisions in response to prayer and obedience, in order to accomplish every minute detail in the panoramic purpose and sweeping counsel of His will (Ephesians 1:11).

The articulate Puritan preacher Thomas Watson described the fascinating doctrine of providence in his characteristic eloquence:

> The providences of God are sometimes dark, and our eyes dim, and we can hardly tell what to make of them; but when we cannot unriddle providence, let us believe that it will work together for the good of the elect (Rom. 8:28). The wheels in a clock seem to move contrary one to the other, but they help forward the motion of the clock, and make the larum strike; so the providences of God seem to be cross wheels; but for all that, they shall carry on the good of the elect. [1]

Some may balk at the thought of a "micromanaging interference" in their lives. They may feel that it impinges on their free will or personal responsibility. But this is where the doctrine of providence hands the baton over to its sister doctrine, that of concurrence.

Concurrence

To the undiscerning eye, a ballpeen hammer and a flathead hammer look like the same tool; they both whack things. They both look equally different from a screwdriver or a tape measure. And yet in the hands of a skilled workman, these two tools are used for vastly different purposes. Since providence and concurrence are both operations of God within the laws of nature, they look equally different from miracles, and yet they are distinct tools in God's collection.

Concurrence is when God *uses human will* to accomplish His purposes.

The classic example of concurrence in the Old Testament is when Joseph's brothers decided to sell him as a slave. After an arduous adventure that included indentured servitude and incarceration, Joseph found himself promoted to chief-of-staff in the Pharaoh's court, armed with inside information, and serendipitously in charge of Egypt seven years before a crippling famine struck the region. When his brothers expressed their reasonable doubt that Joseph would be forgiving of their inexcusable decision, Joseph responded serenely, "As for you, you meant evil against me, but God meant it for good, to bring it about that many people should be kept alive, as they are today" (Genesis 50:20).

In the New Testament, an even more pointed example is described in Peter's fiery Pentecost sermon: "This Jesus, delivered up according to the definite plan and foreknowledge of God, you crucified and killed by the hands of lawless men" (Acts 2:23). How did Jesus end up on the cross? The Jewish religious leaders *plotted* to assassinate Him, Judas *decided* to make a quick buck by betraying his friend, Pilate *permitted* an innocent man to be executed, the Roman soldiers *nailed* Him to a cross, Jesus *gave up* His spirit, and all the while those decisions were all 100 percent "according to the definite plan and foreknowledge of God."

Amazing.

This may feel to you like grappling with a Rubik's Cube. As soon as you get one side clear in your mind, you have scrambled the other side. How can man's sinful decisions be a part of a holy God's plan? To alleviate this tension, theologians sometimes distinguish between God's commands and His permissive decrees. The former are His revealed will for us—for example, "Thou shalt not…," and the latter are what He allows to happen for the ultimate good of man and for His glory.

Thomas Watson again aptly framed this teaching in a picturesque description, saying,

"When a man rides on a lame horse, his riding is the cause why the horse goes, but the lameness is from the horse itself. Herein is God's wisdom, that the sins of men carry on His work, yet He has no hand in them…" [2]

And,

> while [the wicked] disobey His command, they fulfill His permissive decree. If a man sets up two nets, one of silk, the other of iron, the silken net may be broken, not the iron; so while men break the silken net of God's command, they are taken in the iron net of His decree; while they sit backward to God's precepts, they row forward to His decrees. [3]

Concurrence is a tool of God that we do well to recognize. When another person's decision affects our lives, we can rest in the knowledge that they are instruments in God's capable hands. Or as stated in the wisdom of the Proverbs, "The king's heart is a stream of water in the hand of the LORD; he turns it wherever he will" (Proverbs 21:1).

A Good Kind of Interference

Sometimes God uses miracles, as when He destroyed 185,000 Assyrians by deploying an angel of death; at other times, God wields His implements of providence and concurrence just as deftly, as when He harnessed the Babylonian king's decision to invade Nineveh, and a simultaneous, well-timed flooding of the Tigris to again wipe out the Assyrians (Nahum 2). All three are examples of His handiwork, and all are equally amazing. Two are workaday methods of God's involvement in creation, and one is exceedingly rare. And yet all God's methods should be recognizable to those who enjoy praising Him for His provision, help, and grace.

Some Christians, in the sincere desire to prove God's involvement in their life, promote a different type of God's working to the status of miracle, but thus they unintentionally demote the extraordinary nature of God's signs and wonders. So in the quest to prove that God still performs miracles as a normative part of the Christian experience, they redefine miracles to include a plethora of other ways God works.

For example, they call it a miracle when they receive provision of a last-minute reprieve from rent that is due, when actually that is providence. Or they thank God for the long-shot court decision that went in their favor by calling it a miracle when more precisely it is an example of concurrence. I don't mean to be the vocabulary police here, but it is important to distinguish the different varieties of God's involvement in our lives so that we give proper glory to God.

The reason black hat hackers are such an ominous threat to cyberspace is because they don't have our interests at heart—and because they tend to be creepy, disheveled guys who live with their moms and rant about The Man. But when your computer refuses to comply with your wishes, your programs keep crashing, and viruses are persistently prying into your motherboard, wouldn't it be neat to have a white hat hacker skillset in the family? Say a tech-savvy brother-in-law who can remotely hack into your computer and, in five minutes, sort out all your digital woes *and* set up a guard against future hassles?

The power to interfere can be a very desirable trait in an acquaintance who is on your side. The good news is that God is good, He is willing and able to get involved in every nook and cranny of His creation. He wants to do you good, make you Christlike, save your soul, and accompany you on your journey to glory. This is a God you want on your team, and His incomparable power to hack into the matrix of life is what gives you peace and confidence in a world riddled with the effects of sin's curse.

Test claims of miracles, recognize providence, and respect concurrence. These are God's tools for working in God's world. The more you understand them, the less scary they become.

Several poisonous ingredients put together, being tempered by the skill of the pharmacist, make a sovereign medicine, and work together for the good of the patient. So all God's providences, being divinely tempered and sanctified, work together for the best to the saints. He who loves God and is called according to His purpose, may rest assured that everything in the world shall be for his good.

Thomas Watson, *All Things for Good* (Carlisle, PA: Banner of Truth Trust, 2001), 11. First published in 1663 as *A Divine Cordial*

As the elements, though of contrary qualities, yet God has so tempered them that they all work in a harmonious manner for the good of the universe. Or as in a watch, the wheels seem to move contrary one to another, but all carry on the motions of the watch: so things that seem to move cross to the godly, yet by the wonderful providence of God work for their good.

Watson, *All Things for Good,* 25

Jacob wrestled with the angel, and the hollow of Jacob's thigh was out of joint. This was sad; but God turned it to good, for there he saw God's face, and there the Lord blessed him. *'Jacob called the name of the place Peniel, for I have seen God face to face' (Gen. 32:30).* Who would not be willing to have a bone out of joint, so that he might have sight of God?

Watson, *All Things for Good,* 26

Afflictions to the godly are medicinal. Out of the most poisonous drugs God extracts our salvation. Afflictions are as needful as ordinances *(I Peter 1:6).* No vessel can be made of gold without fire; so it is impossible that we should be made vessels of honor, unless we are melted and refined in the furnace of affliction. *'All the paths of the Lord are mercy and truth' (Psalm 25:10).* As the painter intermixes bright colors with dark shadows, so the wise God mixes mercy with judgment.

Watson, *All Things for Good,* 26

The most dark, cloudy providences of God have some sunshine in them. What a blessed condition is a true believer in! When he dies, he goes to God; and while he lives, everything shall do him good. Affliction is for his good.

Watson, All Things for Good, 56

Spiritual good things work for hurt to the wicked. From the flower of heavenly blessings they suck poison. The ministers of God work for their hurt. The same wind that blows one ship to heaven blows another ship upon a rock. The same breath in the ministry that blows a godly man to heaven, blows a profane sinner to hell. They who come with the word of life in their mouths, yet to many are a savor of death.

Watson, All Things for Good, 58

UNCONDITIONAL ELECTION

Curing the Vertigo

MIKE ABENDROTH

Last summer I took my family to the Santa Cruz Beach Boardwalk in California. Our annual pilgrimage always has us finding our way to the cotton candy and the very cool, old-fashioned roller coaster named the Giant Dipper. But we decided to try something different last year. I took my ten- and twelve-year-old daughters to an attraction that allows groups of people to slowly walk through a labyrinthine building replete with odd rooms designed to disorient the paying customers.

The two most discombobulating rooms were what I call the Swirling Room and the Floor Dropping Room. The Swirling Room was actually a long, cylindrical tube with a narrow pathway through the center of it. But the tube was rapidly spinning clockwise, and it was painted black and white with a bizarre swirl pattern straight from the Alfred Hitchcock movie *Vertigo*. The room created the sensation that I was going to topple headlong with two children clutching my legs like vice grips.

The Floor Dropping Room distracted us with all kinds of loud sounds from sources unknown, and just when we thought we were going to exit the room unscathed, the entire floor, hydraulically operated, dropped about six inches. For some reason, with all the special effects, the drop felt more like six yards. Maybe the room should be called the Stomach in Your Throat room because that's the sensation it delivered.

When Christians today hear about the doctrine of election for the first time, they often get the woolies, just as I did that night at the Beach Boardwalk. Minds spinning. Stomachs churning. Does unconditional election have to strike vertiginous feelings in the hearts of Christians? Must predestination evoke a complete mental shutdown due to its woozy implications? Rather than running from the doctrine of unconditional election, which is what many do, allow me to help you to grasp what God's Word says about it, and then we can revel in the glorious grace of our triune God.

In this chapter, I hope to alleviate any negative reaction to election you might have. First, I'll define the term. Next, we'll look at reasons why people find it chilling. And finally, I'll offer some reasons for embracing election as a demonstration of the marvelous grace and matchless love of God. I sincerely hope you will grasp what God's Word says about this teaching. If you do, God's sovereign grace displayed in election will bring Him praise and give you comfort and stability. The Bible will cure your spiritual lightheadedness and disequilibrium concerning the doctrine of election.

What Is Election?

Everyone believes the doctrine of election, depending on the definition. How so? Read the following verses, and you'll see either the exact word or the concept. *Election* and *predestination* are Bible words. All Christians acknowledge that.

> Blessed be the God and Father of our Lord Jesus Christ, who has blessed us in Christ with every spiritual blessing in the heavenly places, even as *he chose us* in him before the foundation of the world, that we should be holy and blameless before him. In love *he predestined us* for adoption through Jesus Christ, according to the purpose of his will, to the praise of his glorious grace, with which he has blessed us in the Beloved...

> In him we have obtained an inheritance, *having been predestined* according to the purpose of him who works all things according to the counsel of his will (Ephesians 1:3-6,11).

> For those whom he foreknew *he also predestined* to be conformed to the image of his Son, in order that he might be the firstborn among many brothers. And those *whom he predestined* he also called, and those whom he called he also justified, and those whom he justified he also glorified (Romans 8:29-30).

God, before time began, freely chose to lavish some people with grace and save them from their sins. The Greek word for *chose* means "to pick out of a group, to select." Unconditional election stresses that God's choice does not depend upon any goodness in the person God chooses.

The Canons of Dort defined election with great detail.

> Election is the unchangeable purpose of God whereby, before the foundation of the world, out of the whole human race, which had fallen by its own fault out of its original integrity into sin and perdition, He has, according to the sovereign good pleasure of His will, out of mere grace, chosen in Christ to salvation a definite number of specific persons, neither better nor more worthy than others, but involved together with them in a common misery. He has also from eternity appointed Christ to be the Mediator and Head of all the elect and the foundation of salvation and thus He decreed to give to Christ those who were to be saved, and effectually to call and draw them into His communion through His Word and Spirit. He decreed to give them true faith in Him, to justify them, to sanctify them, and, after having powerfully kept them in the fellowship of His Son, finally to glorify them, for the

demonstration of His mercy and the praise of the riches of His glorious grace.[1]

Why Does Election Make People Light-Headed?

Here are a few reasons why election makes people a little weak in the knees and spiritually dizzy.

First, election stresses that salvation is completely out of our hands. It strips away our control of redemption just as fast as most fathers grab the television remote from their children. We love to be in control, or at least we want to be under the illusion that we are. Election strips away every last vestige of control in the most important area of life—deciding who goes to God's heaven.

Second, the truth of election pushes the Christian to ask, "What if my loved one isn't chosen? Does that mean that he can never be forgiven and that he is barred from heaven no matter what he does or doesn't do?"

Third, our culture, both secular and sacred, has aggressively promoted the free will of mankind at the expense of the free will of God Himself. (Byron discusses this concept in detail in chapter 3.)

Fourth, it is my scary experience that most Christians today, especially in the West, have been misinformed about election and therefore automatically recoil from it.

Let's examine three biblical facts about election that will cure your spiritual vertigo and firmly establish your soul. Drugs or ear surgery may cure physical vertigo, but the reeling and rocking caused by the initial introduction to unconditional election can be healed by the Bible itself.

Election Reveals the Character of God

God chooses people because election is consistent with the character of the triune Lord. The Bible reveals God's nature, and at His core, He is One who chooses. God discriminates. The Creator selects some while passing over others. The apostle Paul, quoting Exodus 33:19, declares in Romans 9:15, "For he says to Moses, 'I will have mercy on whom I have mercy, and I will have compassion on whom I have compassion.'" In other words, God does whatever He wants to do, including giving mercy and compassion to a select group. How amazing God is for choosing any sinner! Romans 9:15 does not expressly designate the people God will be merciful and compassionate toward. Paul wants all our concentration to be on the Lord who chooses, not on the people He chooses. The Holy Spirit has Paul use an idiom, termed *idem per idem*, which highlights the freedom of God's choice by leaving the action inexact. By using this figure of speech, Paul shows the reader that God is not prejudiced by anything or anyone when He chooses. The stress is on His free choice. What God chooses to do, He does independently and freely.

Paul quotes Exodus 33:19 because he wants the reader to remember the mercy of God, specifically when Israel became an idolatrous calf-worshipping people. God assassinated only 3000 mutineers because He is gracious and merciful to people He has sovereignly chosen to forgive. Actually, Exodus 33:17-23 teaches that at God's core or essence, He desires to sovereignly bestow compassion and grace.

> And the LORD said to Moses, "This very thing that you have spoken I will do, for you have found favor in my sight, and I know you by name." Moses said, "Please show me your glory." And he said, "I will make all my goodness pass before you and will proclaim before you my name 'The LORD.' And I will be gracious to whom I will be gracious, and will show mercy on whom I will show mercy. But," he said, "you cannot see my face, for man shall not see me and live." And the LORD said, "Behold, there is a place by me where you shall stand on the rock, and while my glory passes by I will put you in a cleft of the rock, and I will cover you with my hand until I have passed by. Then I will take away my hand, and you shall see my back, but my face shall not be seen."

Don't be confounded when you grasp that God is, by nature, free to choose. We humans, who are image bearers of God, like to choose as well. Humans choose jobs, spouses, houses, and a myriad of other things. Men and women love to choose. Why? Our hankering to choose reflects God's image.

Election Is the Most Loving Doctrine in the Bible

The most common grievance levied against the doctrine of God's unrestricted and free election is that it is not loving. But the Bible simply says, "In love he predestined us" (Ephesians 1:4-5). What does it mean to you when someone says, "I love you"? When my girlfriend Kim, who is now my bride of 22 years, first said, "Mike, I love you," I was thrilled. Overflowing with joy, I probably blubbered some barely intelligible response. Her words to me were literally breathtaking. How much more should we who are Christians feel our hearts jump for joy when we remember how God loves us? Ephesians 1:4-5 teaches that God's motivation for predestination was love. The phrase "in love" "expresses God's attitude to his people when he foreordained them for adoption into his family." [2] God predestined individuals for the same reason He chose Israel—"It is because the Lord loves you" (Deuteronomy 7:8). If you reject divine election, you undermine His love.

What does it do for your soul when you consider that God would love you? God expresses His love for the Christian in many ways, but never forget the love of God displayed in predestination.

As God says in the Old Testament, "I will heal their apostasy; I will love them *freely*, for my anger has turned from them" (Hosea 14:4). Election means that God chose to love you before time began. Predestination demonstrates God's love, so you must never consider God's love as arbitrary. Love is the reason you are a Christian. Love is the motive for God's choosing. Love from eternity past releases the Christian from the rat race of trying to earn God's favor. Critics slam predestination as capricious, but Paul is only positive about election. Never twist the Scripture so that God's elective love is misrepresented as a negative.

The Greek word for "predestination" in Ephesians 1:4-5 means to "pre-encircle," or to "pre-horizon," meaning "to determine beforehand." It is used only of God in the New Testament. [3] Before Genesis 1:1, God marked out a select group to be saved and forgiven. He determined to know people "beforehand." Let's make it more personal—if you are saved, God knew you in eternity past. Wow! Only God existed before time began, so He alone initiated His love for us.

Ephesians 1:4 clearly indicates when the choice was made. "He chose us in him before the foundation of the world." John Newton often said that if God had not chosen him before time began, He never would have chosen him afterward. Ephesians 1:4 is not a scriptural aberration because the Bible is chock-full of the language of election.

> We should always give thanks to God for you, brethren beloved by the Lord, because God has chosen you from the beginning for salvation through sanctification by the Spirit and faith in the truth (2 Thessalonians 2:13 NASB).

> Do not be ashamed of the testimony about our Lord, nor of me his prisoner, but share in suffering for the gospel by the power of God, who saved us and called us to a holy calling, not because of our works but because of his own purpose and grace, which he gave us in Christ Jesus before the ages began (2 Timothy 1:8-9).

Before you were born, before you did anything right or wrong, before you believed in Jesus Christ, God chose you in eternity past. The theological implication is simple—God's choice in election and predestination was free and sovereign. God chose you because He wanted to. There is no other explanation. It pleased God to love you. Are you smiling yet, or are you still dizzy? John Calvin said, "The very time of election shows it to be free; for what could we have deserved, or in what did our merit consist, before the world was made?" [4]

Election Is Mandatory
Because Humans Are Spiritually Depraved

Many believe election has God looking down the corridor of time and then choosing those who believe the Lord Jesus. That is, God chooses those who first chose Him. "Pre-destiny" then turns into "post-destiny," because in that scheme, God determines the destiny of each person "post" eternity past, based on what the person did or did not do.

But God has never learned anything, because He is gloriously omniscient. In eternity, God did not learn that someone would choose on his or her own to believe. Why? Adam's fall. The main reason people don't understand election is that they underestimate Adam's fall and what it did to the human race. A.W. Pink offers insight to the ramifications of this unbiblical thinking. "To say that salvation turns upon the sinner's own acceptance of Christ would be like offering a sum of money to a blind man upon the condition that he would see." [5]

If God, in eternity past, looked into the future (which He could certainly do), what would He see? Would He see people from various races believing in Jesus and repenting of their sins—all on their own accord? Apart from the Holy Spirit's work in salvation, God would only see sin, depravity, works righteousness, and rebellion. The key that unlocks the understanding is the doctrine of man's inability to please God on his own. In other words, man cannot save himself, so God had to design and achieve the ultimate search and rescue plan. Spurgeon, who always seemed to have a way with words, hollered, "If left to ourselves, the road to hell would be as naturally our choice as for a piece of inanimate matter to roll downwards, instead of assisting itself upwards." [6]

Read the following verses describing the moral corruption of mankind.

> What then? Are we Jews any better off? No, not at all. For we have already charged that all, both Jews and Greeks, are under sin, as it is written:
>
> "None is righteous, no, not one;
>> no one understands;
>> no one seeks for God.
> All have turned aside; together they have become worthless;
>> no one does good,
>> not even one."
> "Their throat is an open grave;
>> they use their tongues to deceive."
> "The venom of asps is under their lips."
>> "Their mouth is full of curses and bitterness."

"Their feet are swift to shed blood;
    in their paths are ruin and misery,
    and the way of peace they have not known."
"There is no fear of God before their eyes" (Romans 3:9-18).

Man is not as horrible as he could be ("utterly depraved"), but he is spiritually unable to save himself. Man's heart, soul, and mind have become dark and debased.

> Now this I say and testify in the Lord, that you must no longer walk as the Gentiles do, in the futility of their minds. They are darkened in their understanding, alienated from the life of God because of the ignorance that is in them, due to their hardness of heart. They have become callous and have given themselves up to sensuality, greedy to practice every kind of impurity (Ephesians 4:17-19).

If you do not believe in unconditional election, it is because you have a problem grasping the depravity of man and what happened when our federal head, Adam, sinned. The solution to your mental difficulties with a God selecting some is found in the moral corruptness of man. If man were good enough to save himself, the crucifixion was a cruel execution of the Son for no reason at all. Spiritually dead people need to be made alive by a sovereign act of God Himself.

> You were dead in the trespasses and sins in which you once walked, following the course of this world, following the prince of the power of the air, the spirit that is now at work in the sons of disobedience—among whom we all once lived in the passions of our flesh, carrying out the desires of the body and the mind, and were by nature children of wrath, like the rest of mankind (Ephesians 2:1-3).

When did God decide to save some Christians? Before the dawn of time. And just think, no one deserved the grace of election. Not one fallen angel was given grace, and God was still God. But the good news for sinners is that God loves rebellious sinners so much that He sent His Son Jesus to die for the ones the Father chose. Amazing love.

I encourage you to follow the apostle Paul's example in regard to election. He is a good model for the believer's attitude with this stressful truth.

Submit to Scripture

Paul was a man of one book. He was fully convinced of the God-breathed nature of Holy Scripture (2 Timothy 3:16-17). God would never put something in Scripture that was not profitable for us or insert doctrines that would harm His people. John Calvin knew that whatever was in the Bible was supposed to be there and that it was good for the readers.

> Scripture is the school of the Holy Spirit, in which, as nothing is omitted that is both necessary and useful to know, so nothing is taught but what is expedient to know. Therefore we must guard against depriving believers of anything disclosed about predestination in Scripture, lest we seem either wickedly to defraud them of the blessing of their God or to accuse and scoff at the Holy Spirit for having published what it is in any way profitable to suppress...But for those who are so cautious or fearful that they desire to bury predestination in order not to disturb weak souls—with what color will they cloak their arrogance when they accuse God indirectly of stupid thoughtlessness as if he had not foreseen the peril that they feel they have wisely met? Whoever, then, heaps odium upon the doctrine of predestination openly reproaches God, as if he had unadvisedly let slip something hurtful to the church.[7]

Praise the Lord Until You Get Dizzy

Paul lifts up election as the first reason to praise God the Father. Before he praises the Father for the redemption of sins through Christ Jesus' work (Ephesians 1:7-12) and for the Holy Spirit's work in sealing the Christian (verses 13-14), Paul blesses the Father for election and predestination.

> Blessed be the God and Father of our Lord Jesus Christ, who has blessed us in Christ with every spiritual blessing in the heavenly places, even as he chose us in him before the foundation of the world, that we should be holy and blameless before him. In love he predestined us for adoption through Jesus Christ, according to the purpose of his will, to the praise of his glorious grace, with which he has blessed us in the Beloved (verses 3-6).

The Greek word translated *blessed* in Ephesians 1:3 closely resembles our word *eulogy*. Paul acclaims the grace of God employing a Jewish style called a *berakah* (blessing). In the New Testament, the word *blessed* is used only of God. Paul has been forgiven for about 25 years by the time he writes this, yet he still bursts forth with worship to the triune God. His salvation experience on the Damascus road was extraordinary. In the Greek, Ephesians 1:3-14 is one single sentence, and it has no main verb (the implied verb is *be*). Paul's lengthy sentence contains 202 Greek words, all screaming praise to God and inviting you to join in. Calvin reflects on Paul's single-mindedness: "The lofty terms in which he extols the grace of God toward the Ephesians, are intended to rouse their hearts to gratitude, to set them all on flame, to fill them even to overflowing with this disposition."[8] When was the last time you praised God specifically for choosing you? Take a moment right now and thank God for electing you. Your head just might stop spinning.

INSIGHTS FROM THE PAST

Therefore, in order to keep the legitimate course in this matter, we must return to the word of God, in which we are furnished with the right rule of understanding. For Scripture is the school of the Holy Spirit, in which as nothing useful and necessary to be known has been omitted, so nothing is taught but what it is of importance to know. Everything, therefore delivered in Scripture on the subject of predestination, we must beware of keeping from the faithful, lest we seem either maliciously to deprive them of the blessing of God, or to accuse and scoff at the Spirit, as having divulged what ought on any account to be suppressed. Let us, I say, allow the Christian to unlock his mind and ears to all the words of God which are addressed to him, provided he do it with this moderation—viz. that whenever the Lord shuts his sacred mouth, he also desists from inquiry...The danger which they dread is not so great that we ought on account of it to turn away our minds from the oracles of God.

John Calvin, *Institutes of the Christian Religion*, chapter 21

DISCERNING
THE VOICE OF GOD

I Hear Voices

MIKE ABENDROTH

Contemporary researchers are hot on the trail of paranormal phenomena. Audio recorders supposedly capture sounds called electronic voice phenomena (EVP). Why the voices are not audible during the time of the recording remains a mystery, but upon playback, with a little post-production filtering, voices are supposedly heard—that is, if you count "oooohhhh" and "weeeaooo" as voices. *Boo!*

Do alternative dimensions actually reveal voices? Some EVP do-it-yourselfers believe their own homes are the best locales to capture ghost noises and voices (and they save gas by not having to drive to Amityville). EVP gurus instruct their students to turn on the recorder and then say, "Good evening. It's nine p.m., and I welcome all spirits." Repeat the last sentence with your scariest voice. Don't forget to heed their most important instruction—you must imagine a force field around yourself so that unfriendly ghosts cannot harm you. (What a bunch of mind games!)

Walk into many evangelical churches today, and you will hear the members talk in a way similar to EVP practitioners—kind of spooky and a wee bit scary. You are likely to hear phrases like these: "I speak in tongues," "I have a private prayer language," and "God told me

_____." If I were a new Christian and entered a church where people said they were hearing directly from God Himself, I would be disquieted and maybe alarmed. Certainly intimidated and inadequate. Many Christians say they hear God speak in a "still small voice," but in the mind of the new church attendee, it could just as well be perceived as God bellowing to members in a "raucous large voice" through rock-concert-sized speakers.

Mormons wrote about "burnings in their bosoms," Quakers listened to their inner light, and Shakers heard from God as they whirled like dervishes, spinning and shaking so as to create a centrifugal conversation with God. Why are evangelical Protestants mimicking these peripheral groups?

Does God speak outside of His Word today? What are we to make of dreams, visions, or inaudible signs? Are "liver shivers" reliable? Are evangelical EVPs infallible? Can such signs be tested or confirmed? Is *The Voice* more than a reality television show? If a person said to you, "God told me you should…" but did not quote a chapter and verse from the Bible, would you believe him? Should you believe him? What does the doctrine of *sola scriptura* tell us about God speaking outside of His Word or in addition to it?

Mysticism is alive and well in most churches today. Disney Movies regularly teach us to trust our hearts, but God's Word regularly warns against such decision-making folly. Jeremiah 17:9 is emphatic: "The heart is deceitful above all things, and desperately sick; who can understand it?" Solomon warns us, "Whoever trusts in his own mind is a fool, but he who walks in wisdom will be delivered" (Proverbs 28:26). Trusting your own heart is not commendable. There is no magic in the kingdom of God! Christian maturity flees from naive self-trust and seizes the sure Word. Instead of placing confidence in others or ourselves, we should follow Solomon's advice:

> Trust in the LORD with all your heart,
>   and do not lean on your own understanding.
> In all your ways acknowledge him,
>   and he will make straight your paths.

Be not wise in your own eyes;
>   fear the LORD, and turn away from evil
(Proverbs 3:5-7).

There are ultimately just two religions in the world—the religion that relies on God's Word alone as the infallible source of revelation and as an external source of guidance, and the religion that looks inwardly for truth, guidance, and leading. Christianity is a revealed religion, not derived from tainted man. Scripture is outside of us. It comes to us from God and is therefore always sure and reliable. Princeton theologian B.B. Warfield demonstrated the antithetical nature of Scripture and mystic experiences.

> Revealed religion comes to man from without; it is imposed upon him from a source superior to his own spirit. The unrevealed religions, on the other hand, flow from no higher source than the human spirit itself...
>
> Evangelical Christianity interprets all religious experience by the normative revelation of God recorded for us in the Holy Scriptures, and guides, directs, and corrects it from these Scriptures, and thus molds it into harmony with what God in His revealed Word lays down as the normal Christian life. The mystic, on the other hand, tends to substitute his religious experience for the objective revelation of God recorded in the written Word, as the source from which he derives his knowledge of God, or at least to subordinate the expressly revealed Word as the less direct and convincing source of knowledge of God to his own religious experience. The result is that the external revelation is relatively depressed in value, if not totally set aside...
>
> There is nothing more important in the age in which we live than to bear constantly in mind that all the Christianity of Christianity rests precisely on "external authority."[1]

You will never go wrong if you build your life on Scripture and let it guide you. Conversely, if you dabble in trusting your inner voices (do men have female inner voices, like my GPS?), feelings, or other

subjective phenomena, heartache will be your portion. A double helping of grief awaits if you abandon the primacy and preeminence of the
Word of God. All sides of the theological controversy agree that the
Word must be central. Why leave the rock of God's Word and wander
off into a potentially hazardous field replete with quicksand lairs and
booby traps? On the drive to the top of Pike's Peak, do you see how
near the edge of the cliff you can drive, or do you hug the safe, inner
side of the road?

The Heart of the Issue

The issues of mystical theology are too complex to navigate completely in a short chapter, but we can quickly establish the sufficiency
of the Word of God and examine everything in light of the competence
of Scripture. My goal is to show you that since the Bible is God's complete and adequate Word, there is no need for God to say anything else.
The next time someone tries to tell you that they have heard "the voice"
(and isn't talking about Andrea Bocelli), you will know exactly what to
do—place no confidence in the "revelation." When you hear someone
allude to the fact that God is communicating with him or her outside
of Scripture, you can rest assured that you are not missing out on anything. You can know for certain that there is something more certain
than what the person is saying. Is God telling me that you must read
this chapter? No, He is not. But I am telling you that you will find the
chapter beneficial.

More Sure

Second Peter 1 describes one of the wildest scenes in all of God's
Word. The lesson to be learned is simple: God's Word is to be trusted
above personal experience, even real and historical experiences (let
alone a made-up dream or a vision caused by late-night frijoles). The
sequential ordering of truth is extremely important. The cart of experience must not come before the horse of God's Word. What you feel,
think, do, or experience is not the final arbiter of truth. God's Word
trumps what has happened in your life, mind, or feelings. In other
words, God's Word is determinative—your experience is not. You

cannot scripturally say, "Thus and such happened to me; therefore it must be true." Instead, you must analyze your experiences through the lens of God's revealed and fixed Word. Note the way Peter prioritizes Scripture.

> We did not follow cleverly devised myths when we made known to you the power and coming of our Lord Jesus Christ, but we were eyewitnesses of his majesty. For when he received honor and glory from God the Father, and the voice was borne to him by the Majestic Glory, "This is my beloved Son, with whom I am well pleased," we ourselves heard this very voice borne from heaven, for we were with him on the holy mountain. And we have something more sure, the prophetic word, to which you will do well to pay attention as to a lamp shining in a dark place, until the day dawns and the morning star rises in your hearts, knowing this first of all, that no prophecy of Scripture comes from someone's own interpretation. For no prophecy was ever produced by the will of man, but men spoke from God as they were carried along by the Holy Spirit (2 Peter 1:16-21).

What is Peter's point?

Peter is declaring the objective surety of the Word of God. His readers should have confidence and certainty in the Scriptures. For Peter, knowing what God infallibly proclaims can combat false teachers and can help people assess various truth claims and experiences. Here's a CliffsNotes version of Peter's exhortation: The Bible is more reliable than experience. Peter, James, and John were earwitnesses and eyewitnesses, but Peter wrote, "We have something more sure, the prophetic word." More sure than what? More sure and trustworthy than their actual experience on the Mount of Transfiguration! They saw the transfigured Jesus. They heard the Father's affirmation of His beloved Son. Yet Peter emphatically taught that the Word was more reliable. Scripture outplays experience. The Bible is more authentic than any evangelical EVP. (Insert floor creaking sound here.)

The apostle bolsters his argument by emphasizing the divine origin of the Bible. The Holy Spirit moved men to write. Men did not concoct the Bible. The language of the apostle is nautically based. Second Peter 1:21 illustrates that if the men God used to pen Scripture were sailboats, God was the wind, blowing the boat in whatever direction and speed He desired. "Men spoke from God as they were carried along by the Holy Spirit." No wonder Peter wants his readers to pay attention to the Word just as they would to a lamp shining in the pitch darkness! God is the author of Scripture. God's Word is reliable. Men are fallible, and they should not trust themselves or their whims.

What do you follow? Whom do you trust? Jonathan Edwards (an eighteenth-century Christian preacher who is widely acknowledged to be one of America's most important and original philosophical theologians and greatest intellectuals) makes the choice simple. He reportedly wondered why people "leave the guidance of the polar star to follow a jack-o'-lantern." Even if you believe God speaks outside of His Word today, look with assurance toward the North Star of God's Word and away from all other voices. If you are a train lover, think of the Scriptures as the locomotive of your life and your experience as the caboose.

Sola Scriptura

Sola scriptura (Latin for "Scripture alone") is the Reformation doctrine that affirms the sufficiency of Holy Writ. Conversely stated, God's Word has no deficiencies. The Bible not only is inerrant (without errors) but also contains everything needful for the salvation of sinners and sanctification of believers. Everything! *Sola scriptura* emphasizes that all other truths and authorities must be secondary and subservient to God's Word. Scripture is sufficient, and it is final. Martin Luther quipped, "The rule is: The Word of God shall establish articles of faith, and no one else, not even an angel." [2] Nothing must supplant Scripture because God's Word is complete and ample. No specific truths about God or from God are found outside of His Word that are not also found inside it. Creation proclaims general truth about God's nature and character, but Scripture alone reveals what theologians call "special revelation."

In light of *sola scriptura*, why would anyone trust any other self-professed guide? Scripture is adequate, and tradition, mysticism, and "God talking" are not needed. We cannot rightly and fully apprehend God outside of the 66 books of the Bible. The only infallible authority is the Bible, so don't trust anything less than the Word, including what you think God is telling you. If an angel allegedly talks to you or you receive a private "revelation," both are subordinate and subject to the Word. More than that, since God's Word is all you need, the message you received is not needed at all. If the Scriptures are sufficient, why would we need something more? If we are to judge everything by the Scriptures, why do we listen to "God told me" statements? God has clearly said in His Word that it contains everything needed for life and godliness (2 Peter 1:3-4)?

Believing that God talks outside His Word today is no different from believing the doctrine of purgatory or papal supremacy. Why? They all reject *sola scriptura*. *Sola scriptura* guards against subjectivity. It protects against mysticism. It locks out personal opinion. The Bible alone is our authority and must be incorporated into our lives as such. Think about it—God breathed out His Word, so it must be edifying, pure, and truthful.

> All Scripture is breathed out by God and profitable for teaching, for reproof, for correction, and for training in righteousness, that the man of God may be competent, equipped for every good work (2 Timothy 3:16-17).

Whatever the pastor needs to accomplish, Paul says the toolbox is the Bible. "Every good work" means every good work. God did not expect elders and pastors to paddle across the ocean in a life raft equipped with only one oar and some stale water. The Greek language in 2 Timothy 3:16-17 highlights the fact that God loaded the lifeboat of ministry with the supplies His sailors in the church would need. God provided for every contingency. Who in their right mind would want to jump overboard and say goodbye to all of God's provisions? How long can you tread shark-invested water? John MacArthur underscores the disaster of abandoning *sola scriptura*: "Once a congregation or a person sees Scripture as less than the final, complete, infallible authority for faith and life, it has thrown open the door to absolute chaos. Absolute chaos."[3]

Here's Mike's maxim (which I probably learned from someone else): As trust in personal experience increases, the need for a sole source of revelation decreases. Conversely, as trust in the sufficient Word of God increases, the perceived need of experience decreases. Even if you think God speaks to you outside of the Bible, you must grant that the Bible is authoritative, infallible, and sufficient.

Bibliolatry

Do others hurl the invective *bibliolatry* at you? You do not worship a book simply because you believe *sola scriptura* or what is in this chapter. A high view of Scripture should never result in pejorative name-calling, but sadly, people resort to about anything to make their point in our subjective times.

Is it proper to love the Bible? Adore a book? Or The Book? E.Y. Mullins understood the relationship between God and His Word:

> This is not to put the literature in the place of the Redeemer,
> but only to assert that the literature is a necessary medium
> for the transmission to us of a knowledge of Him...
>
> The literature comes as the vehicle of objective truth about
> him and his salvation.[4]

Does the bird-watcher worship his binoculars? Does he abandon them? Of course not. You cannot know God except through the Scriptures. Is anyone perturbed if I put my glasses on so that I can see just how pretty my wife is?

David extolled the greatness of God's Word in Psalm 138:2.

> I bow down toward your holy temple
>   and give thanks to your name for your steadfast love and
>   your faithfulness,
>   for you have exalted above all things
>   your name and your word.

Did you notice the seamless relationship between God's name and His Word? Does Calvin shock you with this declaration? "We owe to Scripture the same reverence which we owe to God because it has proceeded from him alone, and has nothing belonging to man mixed with it." [5] Shocked? Jolted? Take a second to reconsider. Now read Psalm 119:48 and prepare yourself for an electric zap: "I will lift up my hands toward your commandments, which I love, and I will meditate on your statutes." Thunderbolt! After your pulse slows down, revel in the fact that we have the Scriptures, a wonderful gift from a generous God.

Summary

Jesus said, "Blessed rather are those who hear the word of God and keep it!" (Luke 11:28). The Bible does not give us any imperatives to listen to our heart, trust in our intuition, or to listen to a still, small voice. Hear the Word. Keep the Word.

How should you make decisions if the Bible does not directly address your issue? First, study the Bible so that you think with a biblical worldview. ("Your testimonies are my delight; they are my counselors"—Psalm 119:24.) Relate to the universe through this grid—God is the sovereign ruler. The Bible constantly reveals that everything should be done for His glory (1 Corinthians 10:31), so make your decision with His glory in mind.

Second, get wisdom (Proverbs 4:5). Ask God for wisdom ("If any of you lacks wisdom, let him ask God, who gives generously to all without reproach, and it will be given him"—James 1:5) and seek out godly wisdom from others ("Where there is no guidance, a people falls, but in an abundance of counselors there is safety"—Proverbs 11:14).

Third, act. Yes, make a decision. God is your Father, and even if you make what you thought was a wise decision but it turns out badly, God can straighten out your mistake. Trust Him and make a decision. Reread Proverbs 3:5-6. You don't need to look for verbal confirmation from God.

Did you notice that these three decision-making steps are backed up by Bible verses? Where is the Bible verse that says, "Trust in your feelings or impressions, or listen for an audible voice of God"? Don't bother checking your concordance. It's not there.

Theological Decoder

I love technological marvels. When I travel overseas, Google Translate is just a click away. *Sprechen Sie deutsch?* When you travel into the murky and mysterious land of "God told me," the following translator will prove invaluable. I call it Mike's Special *Sola Scriptura* Decoder. Here's how it works. I'll give some examples of what people say (the code), and then I'll show what it actually means.

Code: "God told me."

Meaning: "I really think I should do _____, but I am forgetting that the canon of Scripture is closed and there is no need of further revelation. I want confirmation for my precarious decision, and I'm mistaking my intuition for God's voice. I'm forgetting to follow Proverbs 3:5-6."

Code: "I have a peace about it."

Meaning: "I'm forgetting that Jonah had a real 'peace' but that the peace was in the middle of disobedience (Jonah 1:1-5). I'm not remembering the lack of peace I've felt when I've done God-honoring tasks, such as evangelizing my family and confronting sin. I am forgetting peace is a fruit of actions, not the determiner of them."

Code: "I had a dream."

Meaning: "I just watched a YouTube video on Martin Luther King Jr., and I thought he was the man who nailed the 95 Theses to the Wittenberg door. That spicy food last night caused some wild dreams that I'm mistaking for God's instruction."

Code: "God speaks to me when I pray."

Meaning: "I'm forgetting that God speaks to me through the Bible and I speak to God through prayer (and never the twain shall meet). I'm forgetting that people are often given tranquilizers when they hear hallucinatory voices."

Code: "I heard a still, small voice."
Meaning: "I've forgotten that the Bible describes many situations that are not prescribed for believers today. I've overlooked hermeneutical principles and have extrapolated the entire Bible. I did the same thing with WWJD, forgetting that Jesus did many things that do not apply to me." (Jesus never asked people to pray for Him. Have you?)

Code: "I had a burning in my bosom."
Meaning: "I forgot to take my Tums or Prilosec."

Concluding Recording

I decided to set up an EVP recording device in my basement. With great anticipation, I returned from vacation, and after some high-resolution filtering, I pushed the play button. Amazingly, I heard two distinctly different voices. One sounded German, and the other had a Welsh accent. Here's what they said.

> Feelings come and feelings go
> And feelings are deceiving;
> My warrant is the Word of God,
> Naught else is worth believing.
> —attributed to Martin Luther[6]

> Avoid the mistake of concentrating overmuch upon your feelings. Above all, avoid the terrible error of making them central.
> —D.M. Lloyd-Jones

Let us imagine I follow the mystic way. I begin to have experiences; I think God is speaking to me; how do I know it is God who is speaking to me? How can I know I am not speaking to man; how can I be sure that I am not the victim of hallucinations, since this has happened to many of the mystics? If I believe in mysticism as such without the Bible, how do I know I am not being deluded by Satan as an angel of light in order to keep me from the true and living God? I have no standard... The evangelical doctrine tells me not to look into myself but to look into the Word of God; not to examine myself, but to look at the revelation that has been given to me. It tells me that God can only be known in His own way, the way which has been revealed in the Scriptures themselves.

D. Martyn Lloyd-Jones, *Fellowship with God*
(Wheaton, IL: Crossway Books, 1993), 95

The whole counsel of God, concerning all things necessary for his own glory, man's salvation, faith, and life, is either expressly set down in scripture, or by good and necessary consequence may be deduced from scripture: unto which nothing at any time is to be added, whether by new revelations of the Spirit, or traditions of men.

The Westminster Confession of Faith (1:6)

We believe that the Word contained in these books has proceeded from God, and receives its authority from him alone, and not from men. And inasmuch as it is the rule of all truth, containing all that is necessary for the service of God and for our salvation, it is not lawful for men, nor even for angels, to add to it, to take away from it, or to change it. Whence it follows that no authority, whether of antiquity, or custom, or numbers, or human wisdom, or judgments, or proclamations, or edicts, or decrees, or councils, or visions, or miracles, should be opposed to these Holy Scriptures, but on the contrary, all things should be examined, regulated, and reformed according to them.

The French Confession of Faith (1559), Art. V

COMMITTING TO
CHURCH MEMBERSHIP

Anuptaphobia and the Bride of Christ

CLINT ARCHER

He was new to the creepy little town but not a visitor. This dot on an Appalachian map was now home. His Christian upbringing had left his conscience averse to the solo lobo syndrome. "A lone wolf is a dead wolf," his sagacious grandma warned. So that first Sunday he dutifully visited the only church in town. Its shabby, unkempt exterior didn't put him off. It matched the aging appearance of all the local buildings and their occupants. He wasn't expecting much from the service that morning, but still, something was slightly off-kilter about the experience, as if a painting had been hung askew—just enough to pique one's awareness but not enough to be called crooked.

The bald greeter at the door seemed genuinely happy to meet the stranger. And although he never removed his right hand from the pocket of his suit pants, he warmly gripped the visitor by the shoulder and led him toward the sparse, seated congregation. The tight-knit cohort of a dozen or so regulars greeted him enthusiastically. Everyone was friendly, though one or two could not mask their bemusement that this stranger had chosen to worship with them.

A short elderly lady on well-used crutches peppered him with personal questions regarding his provenance, vocation, and intentions of staying. Her long dress hid the reason for her need of assistance. A smartly dressed, middle-aged gentleman interrupted her barrage of questions, gently announcing that the service was commencing. He then walked with a slight limp to the pulpit. The sermon contained nothing untoward, and the discerning new face smiled approvingly at the literal interpretation and faithfulness to the King James text.

But behind his smile, the man found his thoughts wandering to the strange coincidence that the gentleman in the pew next to him and the young lady sitting across the aisle from him were both missing some fingers.

After the service, as he exited the gravel parking lot, he saw the fellow who had greeted him at the door lugging a trash can. He gripped its handle with his left hand and hugged it to his chest with his right arm, revealing a stump where his hand had been amputated. The flame of curiosity was now unquenchable.

Impulsively pushing the brake pedal, he hopped out, leaving the driver's door open, trotted over to the greeter and blurted, "I'm really sorry if this is rude, but I was wondering…what happened to your hand?" As the words sailed from his mouth, he realized how boorish he was being. He tried to recoup and offered, "It's just that I also noticed a few others in the church who…" He couldn't bring himself to finish. "You know…well, never mind. Sorry for…uh, have a nice day." Just before he turned back to his car, the greeter smiled and said, "If you decide to become a member here, you'll find out."

The Perception of Membership

Churches and denominations teach varying views on church membership. Your perception of membership probably depends on your upbringing, denominational practices, and experience with certain churches. For some, membership seems normal. They belong to a gym, a country club, and a band—why not a church? To others, membership feels intrusive and restrictive, like a spiritual straitjacket. Some churches compound this perception by creating membership requirements as intimidating as a Faustian contract for your soul.

Some church membership requirements border on being illegal.

You would experience this if you decided to visit a church of Appalachian snake handlers, as our unsuspecting stranger did. This quirky sect is renowned, not for its numerical growth but for a disturbing and occasionally lethal worship rite—holding venomous serpents, usually rattlesnakes. (Two hints that you've stumbled upon such a church: the inordinate number of handicapped parking spots and a visibly surprised greeter at the door.)

The Church of God preacher George Went Hensley founded the dubious movement in the 1920s. Tragically, his own wife died of a snakebite. His faith, however, remained resolute to the end, which came in 1955, when at the age of 75, he too died of a snakebite. *Quelle surprise.*

The rationale for this macabre commitment is that people who trust everything in the Word of God should practice everything found there. This includes Luke 10:17-19, where Jesus tells the 72 evangelists, "I have given you authority to tread on serpents and scorpions, and over all the power of the enemy, and nothing shall hurt you." The context clearly refers to the demons they were able to cast out, causing Satan, the serpent of old, to "fall like lightning from heaven." But instead of paying attention to context and employing a modicum of common sense, this small group of believers remain pertinacious in their belief that Christians should handle poisonous snakes as a sign of faith in God's Word.

Although the practice is legal only in West Virginia, there are today about forty churches in the USA and four in Canada that maintain this rite, to date accruing over a hundred fatalities and scores of maimed members who have lost fingers, hands, and legs to the hemotoxic venom of rattlesnakes.

No one can question the movement's evidence of a committed membership. This introduces a pertinent question in the contemporary church scene: Just how committed does a Christian really need to be to become a member of a local church?

On one extreme, you may have a church that has no formal procedure at all. They are like buskers. "Just enjoy the show and leave. A few coins in the coffer would be appreciated. Feel free to get as involved or stay as anonymous as you want. You can sign up for the weekly e-mail if you like, but if you'd rather not, no problem. You can still tell people this is your church."

On the other hand, some churches insist on what feels like an FBI background investigation, weeks of doctrinal classes, signatures with witnesses on a statement of faith and members' covenant, a public testimony, a vociferous congregational discussion...followed by a formal vote of secret ballot and either a triumphant ceremony of acceptance or a humiliating retry at the next meeting. It almost makes the simplicity of a rattlesnake faith test seem attractive.

As always, we need to shelve our perceptions and preconceptions, and examine what the Word of God says on the matter.

The Proof of Membership

Ophidiophobia is an abnormal fear of snakes. I call it common sense. The aversion to churches that require handling venomous vipers is perfectly rational. There are reasons to avoid certain churches, but many who refuse to become church members have no good reason.

I appreciate folks in my church who ask me to produce a chapter and verse for any doctrine I mention. Like the Bereans, they are diligently "examining the Scriptures daily to see if these things were so" (Acts 17:11). I have been asked, "Where in the Bible does God say I need to be a member of a church?" I occasionally like to reply with the playful retort, "Where does the Bible tell wives to love their husbands?" The fact is that some instructions in Scripture, though never overtly stated, are supplied by the implication of other commands. Older women, for example, are told in Titus 2:4 to "train the young women to love their husbands and children." Christians are also told to love their neighbors and their enemies alike. The command for a wife to love her husband is never actually stated, but it is an obvious implication of other commands.

Likewise, though membership is not commanded in any particular verse, dozens of other directives and situations certainly imply it. As Mark Dever and Paul Alexander explain in their excellent work, *The Deliberate Church*, "It may seem like a stretch to say that local church membership is a biblical concept—that is, until we actually start looking for it in the Bible. It's not as pronounced as the atonement or justification by faith. But the evidence is there, and it is consistent."[1] There may be different approaches in methodology, but the leadership of a local church needs a process to distinguish—to borrow the apostle Paul's language from 1 Corinthians 5:12—those inside the church from those outside.

From the many commands in Scripture that imply membership, I see at least five lines of reasoning that prove God's will for Christians is to be formally attached to a local church as opposed to loosely associated.

The Presence of a Majority

Commands addressed to a majority imply some sort of understanding of who constitutes the congregation. In 2 Corinthians 2:5-6 Paul says to the Corinthian church, "Now if anyone has caused pain, he has caused it not to me, but in some measure—not to put it too severely—to all of you. For such a one, this punishment by the majority is enough." The fact that Paul and the church at Corinth recognized a majority showed that they knew how many people constituted their local body.

In Acts 6:2 the apostles summoned "the full number of the disciples" in their embryonic megachurch of 5000. They knew how many were in their church and when the full number was gathered. Also, delegates delivered a letter to the church at Antioch only when the whole church was gathered (Acts 15:30).

The Ability to Remove Members

The command to discipline believers by removing them from a church implies that the congregation is aware of who is inside and who is outside the church. In Matthew 18 Jesus supplied directions on how to graciously and patiently purge the church of unrepentant members. In the penultimate step, "If he refuses to listen to [two or three witnesses], tell it to the church." The final step had to be taken before *the* assembly, not *an* assembly. Not an ad hoc committee, but the church. It seems reasonable to assume that there was knowledge of who constituted that church. And in the final step, "If he refuses to listen even to the church, let him be to you as a Gentile and a tax collector," another action for the entire assembly to be involved in. Discipline does not work without the cooperation of the entire church.

Similarly, in the church at Corinth, a church discipline case was brewing. The offending brother had been committing acts of unrepentant indecency, and Paul told the church not to allow him to remain as part of the assembly, but to put him out. Paul employed very specific language to differentiate between those inside and those outside. "What have I to do with judging outsiders? Is it not those inside the church whom you are to judge? God judges those outside. 'Purge the evil person from among you'" (1 Corinthians 5:12-13; see also 2 Thessalonians 3:14).

The Consensus of Who Is in the Church

The commands to choose from within the church imply a knowledge of who the members were. For example, in Acts 6:3 the apostles instructed the fully assembled church to select the first seven deacons from among the disciples—not from outside the church, but from within it. No outside hires would be accepted. It stands to reason that the church was aware of who qualified as an insider. This principle of who is "among you" is reinforced by the practice of sending letters of commendation and acceptance with perambulating believers who visited new congregations (for example, see Acts 18:26-27; Colossians 4:10).

There are also lists of widows in the church who were eligible for support. "Let a widow be enrolled if she is not less than sixty years of age, having been the wife of one husband" (1 Timothy 5:9). The term *enrolled* means to be added to a list. There was an understanding of which widows were the responsibility of which church.

Also, the church was responsible for the support of its pastor (see 1 Corinthians 9:4-14). This implies a consensus of who was responsible to support which pastor.

Corporate Commands

The ubiquitous "one another" commands in the New Testament imply that believers are in congregations of people whom they are to serve, admonish, encourage, stir up to love and good deeds, help bear burdens, and so on. These commands are not referring to the community in general, but always to people in the church. Having a formal membership list helps us know whom we are to target when obeying these commands.

Accountability of Leaders

The commands for elders to be responsible for their flocks imply that they knew who their flocks were. The leadership of the church is commanded to pray for, teach, protect, and rebuke the sheep in the flock. They would obviously need to know to whom they owe this responsibility.

In 1 Peter 5 we read, "Shepherd the flock of God that is among you, exercising oversight, not under compulsion, but willingly, as God would have you; not for shameful gain, but eagerly; not domineering over those in your charge, but being examples to the flock. And when the chief Shepherd appears, you will receive the unfading crown of glory" (1 Peter 5:2-4). The elders' reward is linked to their faithfulness to their charge. A wise shepherd would take seriously knowing for whom he will give an account.

When someone insists on a chapter and verse on membership, I slide Hebrews 13:17 out of my scabbard. This unequivocal instruction cuts to the bone. "Obey your leaders and submit to them, for they are keeping watch over your souls, as those who will have to give an account. Let them do this with joy and not with groaning, for that would be of no advantage to you."

If a church's leadership decides to use a different process, then you may be off the hook. It is conceivable that a small congregation of 12 people would know when someone is attending regularly, wanting accountability, and showing commitment through giving and serving. They may informally decide whether this person is one of them or not, and they would presumably find a way to communicate this to the person.

But if the leaders of the church you attend require membership, then you need to obey them. They will, after all, be accountable for your soul on judgment day. It seems reasonable for them to ask you to make it clear that you expect your name to come up when they give a reckoning for your soul with Jesus.

The Pictures of Membership

Another strong case for formal church membership is as blatant as a bug on a windshield to anyone familiar with the New Testament. The images employed to describe the church irrefutably imply a formal connection, not a loose association.

The Household

The household metaphor emphasizes the bonds of familial strength (1 Peter 4:17). When your five-year-old daughter doesn't show up to the table for dinner, you notice. If your teenage son casually announced that he was transferring to his friend's family, there would be some resistance. The severing of the family bond to start a new family, such as at a wedding, is usually a big deal that includes tears and official documents.

The Flock

The flock metaphor also implies that the good shepherd would know if any of his sheep were missing (1 Peter 5:2). Shepherds frowned on their sheep casually wandering to sample the greener grass in the pasture of another flock.

The Body

The body metaphor speaks for itself (1 Corinthians 12:12-27). But allow me to pose one question: If your thumb looked like it was about to leave your body, would you actively resist that, or would you casually dismiss your connection to that digit as a loose association, merely hoping it would return? Exactly.

The Building

The building metaphor is a vivid picture of strength through formal connection (1 Corinthians 3:10; 1 Peter 2:5). Bricks are affixed with mortar; they are not stacked loosely. If a neighbor came and took a few of your bricks, you would notice and object. The inimitable Charles Spurgeon bewailed the "rolling stone" mentality of those who eschewed membership with these words.

> What is a brick for? To help build a house. It's of no use for a brick to tell you it is just as good a brick while it is kicking about on the ground, as it would be in the house. It is a good-for-nothing brick. So you, rolling stone Christians, I do not believe you are answering your purpose. You are living contrary to the life which Christ would have you live.

The Priority of Membership

In the Danish town of Billund in 1932, Ole Kirk Christiansen began making little wooden blocks as toys for children. These toys developed over the next 26 years into the system of "automatic binding bricks" made of acrylonitrile-butadiene-styrene. A common plastic. They had several round studs on top and a hollow rectangular bottom, enabling them to snap together. The company name comes from the Danish phrase *leg godt*, which means "play well." We call the blocks Legos. Today the production of bricks averages 20 billion per year, or 600 bricks a second. Every person on the planet could own 62.

The genius of the system lies in the way it blends unity and diversity. The bricks are produced according to various themes, including Vikings, pirates, Star Wars, construction workers, and knights of Camelot. But each block is primarily part of a universal system. Despite tremendous variation in the design and purpose of individual pieces over the years, each remains compatible with existing pieces. Bricks from 1958 still interlock with those made today. When snapped together, Lego pieces can't be too easily pulled apart, or the resulting constructions would be unstable. They can't be too difficult to pull apart because the interchangeability with other constructions is part of the appeal.

The similarities with another organization are uncanny. The universal church consists of millions of bricks, or "living stones" (1 Peter 2:5). These bricks have been produced in various countries over many years. They appear in a variety of contexts, whether Baptist, Presbyterian, Anglican, charismatic, conservative, or whatever, but all are first and foremost part of a universal system. And those Christians made in AD 33 are compatible with those made in 2014.

Although Christians are individuals before God and can shift from one congregation to another as they change their domicile, they are useful only if they are snapped together tightly enough to be part of a particular work. As a Christian who is part of the worldwide universal church, you also need to be part of a local congregation. The local church is the manifestation of the universal church. If you are not plugged into a church, you are a rogue believer. The writer of Hebrews outlines your responsibility and gives a warning if you habitually neglect it.

> And let us consider how to stir up one another to love and good works, not neglecting to meet together, as is the habit of some, but encouraging one another, and all the more as you see the Day drawing near.
>
> For if we go on sinning deliberately after receiving the knowledge of the truth, there no longer remains a sacrifice for sins, but a fearful expectation of judgment, and a fury of fire that will consume the adversaries (Hebrews 10:24-27).

Did you get that? You need to be part of a group of Christians who meet together regularly. If you skip a service for vacation, that's one thing. But if you have no desire to meet with fellow believers and you are habitually neglecting the meeting, you are "sinning deliberately," which implies you could be an unbeliever or "adversary" with "a fearful expectation of judgment." Okay, so this is serious stuff. This is why pastor and author Mark Dever, who has taught and written extensively on church membership, often begins his sermon on this topic with these attention-grabbing words: "If you are not a member of the church, you may be going to hell." He goes on to explain that in the same way that a desire to be accountable and to be involved in God's family is a sign of grace, the converse is also true. If you don't want accountability or involvement, what does that say about the state of your soul? Christians are by definition sinners who repent. If you refuse to repent of your neglected involvement of your church, it may be right to question the assurance of your salvation.

Conclusion

Membership can be a scary doctrine. But it's a necessary one for Christians to understand. The fear of committing to a local church is an indicator of spiritual immaturity. It's analogous to another kind of fear of commitment called *anuptaphobia*. Anuptaphobia is an extreme fear of staying single or of being married to the wrong person for life. This type of commitment dysfunction is common among single people who want the benefits of marriage, such as companionship, sex, convenience of cohabitation, and perhaps even children. But they simultaneously crave the freedom of independence. They try to reserve the moral right to bail on the relationship if it suits them to do so. But the benefits of marriage are permissible only within the impenetrable fortress of the marriage covenant. It is commitment that makes marriage work. In the same way, membership opens the door to benefits of the local church.

If you say you love Christ but you hate His bride, you are deluding yourself. If you want to be united to Christ but refuse union with His church, you are advocating spiritual anuptaphobia. It betrays immaturity and confused priorities. Are you the type of person who would commit to a gym but not a church? What does that tell you about your spiritual life?

I love author Joshua Harris's sobriquet for people who like to visit churches but refuse to commit. He calls them "church daters." They are people who test drive churches the way teenage boys try out girlfriends through the serial monogamy of dating. Harris insightfully points out that church daters tend to be "me centered, independent, and critical."[2]

They look for a church that suits their felt needs and that lets them do what they want. But they often find something wrong with the church, which supposedly justifies their reluctance to commit.

Picture an immature guy who dates a young lady because of what he gets out of the relationship. He enjoys the freedom that dating affords as opposed to marriage, and he reserves the right to break it off with her when he thinks he can do better. Nauseating, isn't it? Meet the modern church dater. Is this pathetic portrait a picture of you and your commitment to Christ's bride? As intimidating as it may be, I challenge you to be like your Savior and love the church. Overcome your spiritual anuptaphobia.

INSIGHTS FROM THE PAST

The primary and indispensable qualification for membership in a particular Church, consists in a connection with the general Church, or body of Christ. "Everyone is so far a member of Christ's Church as he is a member of Christ's body." Each particular Church seeks to represent, in itself, the kingdom of Christ, and ought, therefore, to be composed entirely of spiritual materials. It is no part of its design to embrace unbelievers, and prepare them for the kingdom of heaven. They have no right to its privileges and blessings. They are intruders at its ordinances. No ecclesiastical recognition of them as children can change their relation as aliens and strangers; and they who introduce them contravene the declared will of the great Head of the Church. The gates of his kingdom are open to none but converted men. It is, therefore, the imperative duty of the Churches to admit to membership none but such as give satisfactory evidence that they have been born again.

J.L. Reynolds "Church Polity or the Kingdom of Christ" (1849), as cited in Mark Dever, *Polity* (Washington, DC: Center for Church Reform, 2001), 323

The Lord Jesus Christ hath committed the use and power of the keys, in matters of government, to every visible congregational church, to be used, according to the rules and directions that he hath given in his word, in his name, and to his glory. The keys are the power of

Christ, which he hath given to every particular congregation, to open and shut itself by; and to do all things in order to the great things proposed, viz. his glory and his people's spiritual benefit, in peace and purity, Isa. 9:7. and 22:22. Rev. 3:7. Heb. 3:6. Ephe. 2:19–22. Matt. 16:19. John 20:23.

Benjamin Griffith, "A Short Treatise" (1743), as cited in Mark Dever, Polity (Washington, DC: Center for Church Reform, 2001), 99

A Church constituted after the heavenly pattern is as a city set on a hill, from which the glories of rich and free grace abundantly shine, Psalm 50:2. The true members of it have the light of the gospel shining in their hearts, by the Holy Spirit, and are entitled to all the blessings of the new covenant, Eph. 1:3. And being thus blessed, their faith is a lively, active faith, not only purifying their hearts, but working by love, Gal. 5:6, whereby they become the light of the world, Matt. 5:14-16, which they make apparent by a faithful discharge of the duties enjoined them by the Lord Jesus Christ, the great Head of the church, James 2:18.

Charleston Association, "A Summary of Church Discipline" (1774), as cited in Mark Dever, Polity (Washington, DC: Center for Church Reform, 2001), 125

THE LOSS OF
HEAVENLY REWARDS

This May Hurt a Little

CLINT ARCHER

It was a sobering and humiliating punishment. Millions of television viewers watched in morbid fascination as the eight victims of the controversial verdict stood in disbelief, shell-shocked and crestfallen. After the many years of effort and sacrifice, the countless hours of practice and training, the untold expense of sponsorship and support, four womens' doubles pairs were disqualified from the Olympic badminton finals for the crime of...wait for it...not trying hard enough.

Badminton is generally perceived as a placid sport, not known for its drama. But the brouhaha of the "shuttlecock scandal" in the London Olympics in 2012 made history with a bizarre turn of events. Two womens' doubles teams from China, one from South Korea, and one from Indonesia were unceremoniously disqualified for, in the words of the vice president of the International Olympic Committee, Craig Reedie, "not using one's best efforts to win a match." The players had all cleared the elimination round and were apparently attempting to lose their games to attain a more lenient placing in the following round.

The comical self-sabotage was hard to miss. The best female badminton players on the planet were not merely lagging a little in their enthusiasm, but deliberately throwing their matches with double faults.

They were playing with such lackluster effort that the shuttlecock, like a pathetic flightless fowl, repeatedly failed to clear the net. The players made no token pretense at appearing disappointed when they lost a point. But their dastardly antics cost them a shot at Olympic gold.

There is an unfortunate parallel in the spiritual realm. Grace by faith alone is a precious doctrine. But ever since its most popular publication (the book of Romans), professing believers have been tempted to rest on the laurels of free forgiveness instead of striving for heavenly reward. Paul addressed those who would sin under the banner of "once saved always saved" with these unambiguous words: "What shall we say then? Are we to continue in sin that grace may abound? By no means! How can we who died to sin still live in it?" (Romans 6:1-2).

The Olympic badminton disgrace provides an apt parable for the poor service of many Christian lives. Our Lord was fond of revealing real-life snapshots of inept stewardship and its consequences. The New Testament parables are peppered with a cast of stewards who didn't try hard enough (for example, see Matthew 25:26-28; Luke 12:45-46).

To be clear, let's remember that there is no condemnation for those in Christ Jesus (Romans 8:1). Condemnation is the eternal death of hell, the never-ending separation of unrepentant sinners from a holy God. When Jesus lived a perfect life and then offered that righteousness on the cross on behalf of those who would believe, He paid for every sin that would be committed by every person who trusts Jesus for salvation. So why is there a judgment for believers? To answer that, we must understand the different types of judgments.

There is the judgment of unbelievers, a time of God's justice and wrath, based on their deeds of sin and resulting in condemnation. But there is also a judgment of believers, a time of grace and mercy, based on the deeds of Christ and resulting in reward. Scripture refers to this judgment, or rewards ceremony, as the judgment seat (*bēma*) of Christ. At this glorious event, believers will receive their rewards, commendation, and new assignments in the kingdom. But many Christians overlook that this appraisal of our lives will result in varying degrees of reward for varying degrees of faithfulness. This awesome truth may sound scary, but the more we understand of it, the more we will be inspired to be faithful and will anticipate our Master's eternal rewards.

The Master's Degrees:
Understanding Reward at Christ's *Bēma* Judgment

Christians understand that salvation from condemnation is a gift of grace—equally glorious and equally free for all believers, irrespective of when they repent. Our Lord taught this explicitly in the parable of the generous landowner in Matthew 20. The thief on the cross—saved for only a few hours—will enjoy the same salvation from his sins and their consequences as the apostle John, who served Christ for decades. There are no degrees of forgiveness. But does that mean our behavior, words, and motives have no bearing on our eternity whatsoever? Consider these sample warnings, directed at believers.

- "Now if anyone builds on the foundation with gold, silver, precious stones, wood, hay, straw—each one's work will become manifest, for the Day will disclose it, because it will be revealed by fire, and the fire will test what sort of work each one has done. If the work that anyone has built on the foundation survives, he will receive a reward. If anyone's work is burned up, he will suffer loss, though he himself will be saved, but only as through fire" (1 Corinthians 3:12-15). Note that the person who suffers loss due to his faulty foundation is not an unbeliever, but one who will be saved. Paul is talking about believers.

- "Do not pronounce judgment [on other believers] before the time, before the Lord comes, who will bring to light the things now hidden in darkness and will disclose the purposes of the heart. Then each one will receive his commendation from God" (1 Corinthians 4:5). This passage refers to a time after the Lord comes when believers' motives will result in the corresponding commendation from Jesus (reminiscent of the "good and faithful servant" commendation in the parable of the talents in Matthew 25).

- "For we must all appear before the judgment seat [*bēma*] of Christ, so that each one may receive what is due for what he has done in the body, whether good or evil" (2 Corinthians 5:10). Here Paul warns believers (including himself!) that they will receive what is due to them, according to their deeds in this life. The Greek word translated *evil* means "futile or worthless."

- "For it is time for judgment to begin at the household of God; and if it begins with us, what will be the outcome for those who do not obey the gospel of God?" (1 Peter 4:17). Peter is referring to God's discipline of believers—"the household of God"—in this life.

- "It is for discipline that you have to endure. God is treating you as sons. For what son is there whom his father does not discipline?" (Hebrews 12:7).

Believers are not exempt from accountability in this life or the next. Many Christians have a misconception of the day of their judgment. Either they fear that their sins will somehow haunt them by being flashed before them and others on some giant plasma display, or alternatively, they assume blithely that since believers are forgiven of all sins, there will be no accountability for them in the afterlife. Both views are wrong.

The Bible teaches clearly that believers will be rewarded according to their stewardship of God's gifts to them. Their words, deeds, and motives will be scrutinized and will result in eternal reward or the loss of reward. No sin will have any effect on their salvation or their perfect righteousness through Christ. But their rewards will be commensurate and in proportion to their faithful stewardship of the gifts God gave them.

The *bēma* judgment of believers is an appraisal done in love for the purpose of apportioning rewards. On the other hand, the judgment of unbelievers (the Great White Throne judgment of Revelation 20:11) is a reckoning of wrath for the purpose of punishing rebellion. In the one, the outcome is always reward. In the other, it is always condemnation.

Splitting Heirs: Are All Believers Equal in Heaven?

People often ask whether all believers are equal in heaven. Regrettably, I am constrained to offer the most annoying of answers—yes and no.

Yes, in essence and in standing before God, all believers are perfectly equal in heaven. We will be equally clothed in Christ's righteousness. We will all be perfectly content, and there will be no rivalry or comparisons. And yet the functions and roles of believers are not identical.

Although believers are all equally saved, they will have various roles in the afterlife. The apostles provide a clear example of this hierarchy. Jesus offers a promise of unique reward to the 12 apostles. (Presumably Matthias would take Judas's position.)

> You are those who have stayed with me in my trials, and I assign to you, as my Father assigned to me, a kingdom, that you may eat and drink at my table in my kingdom and sit on thrones judging the twelve tribes of Israel (Luke 22:28-30).

The reward includes a function of governing (a throne) and a sphere of responsibility (a kingdom). These are specific to the apostles and not conferred on all believers. This proves that at least 12 believers will have a more privileged function or role in the eternal kingdom. But are they the only ones who will have a special position in eternity?

Suffering Saints:
Can a Believer Really Lose Eternal Reward?

You may agree with the notion that some believers—at least the 12 apostles—have more prominent roles or functions in the kingdom of God, but perhaps you are not yet ready to concede that other believers will lose rewards. It's not the logic alone, however, that indicates that believers can forfeit eternal reward. Biblical evidence demands it.

John wrote, "Watch yourselves, so that you may not lose what we have worked for, but may win a full reward" (2 John 8). In 1 Corinthians 3:15 we are told spiritual leaders who build their ministries out of substandard material will suffer loss. The exact meaning is not given, but I'm sure you will agree that whatever "suffer loss" means, it certainly cannot mean "*not* suffer loss."

Now, let's be clear that there is no purgatorial punishment or chastisement in the afterlife for believers. We are immune from all condemnation because of the full price Jesus paid for our sins. The forfeiture of reward is not punishment. It is simply being assigned the function in heaven that correlates with one's faithful stewardship of God's gifts.

At this point, any good Protestant should be shifting uneasily in his or her seat. We are saved by faith, not works. Salvation is a free gift of God. How can our deeds affect our afterlife if Jesus paid it all? This question reminds us to draw a clear distinction between what we do to be saved (nothing) and what we do once we are saved. In Ephesians 2:10, Paul reminds us that we were saved not *by* good works, but *for* good works.

Prophets of Profit: What Are the Eternal Rewards?

In Scripture, crowns are traditionally synonymous with eternal rewards, and they symbolize more than just glittering headgear. Crowns represent authority and position. The true reward in eternity is the position and responsibility granted to the believer. We will all serve Christ in various capacities. The family business in the kingdom of God is governing. As a child of God and coheir of Christ, the believer's eternity involves ruling and reigning with Christ. This breathtaking privilege is alluded to in many passages and even explicitly promised in a few.

Consider Paul's off-the-cuff comment in which he chides the Corinthians for their inability to settle civil disputes within the church. His rationale for prohibiting outside arbitration is this enigmatic statement: "Do you not know that we are to judge angels? How much more, then, matters pertaining to this life!" (1 Corinthians 6:3). Wait, what? The word *judge* refers to ruling and governing, as in the designation given to the ad hoc rulers of Israel in the book of Judges. We believers will rule angels in the kingdom in some capacity.

Another clue that our eternal reward involves reigning is found in the parable of the minas in Luke 19. The good steward who managed his master's investment faithfully was rewarded with increased authority. "Well done, good servant! Because you have been faithful in a very little, you shall have authority over ten cities" (Luke 19:17).

Explicit references to the ruling function of believers feature prominently in the book of Revelation.

- "Then I saw thrones, and seated on them were those to whom *the authority to judge was committed.* Also I saw the souls of those who had been beheaded for the testimony of Jesus and for the word of God, and those who had not worshiped the beast or its image and had not received its mark on their foreheads or their hands. They came to life and *reigned with Christ* for a thousand years" (Revelation 20:4).

- "Blessed and holy is the one who shares in the first resurrection! Over such the second death has no power, but they will be priests of God and of Christ, and *they will reign with him* for a thousand years" (Revelation 20:6).

- "Night will be no more. They will need no light of lamp or sun, for the Lord God will be their light, and *they will reign* forever and ever" (Revelation 22:5).

The rewards promised by God are frequently referred to in terms of authority. Mostly, the symbols of the rewards are pictured as crowns (2 Timothy 4:8; James 1:12; 1 Peter 5:4; Revelation 2:10; 3:11) and thrones (Matthew 19:28; Revelation 3:21; 4:4).

Whether we receive literal, physical crowns is irrelevant. The point is, functions and positions of authority accompany the reward. The physical tiara awarded to a beauty queen is not the reason she entered the competition. It is merely the symbol of her victory and the prize that comes with the position.

The Score Sheet:
What Are the Criteria for Eternal Rewards?

In our seminary homiletics lab, preaching students delivered messages to a hungry pack of peers. The salivating audience then had the delectable task of critiquing their victim. But the professor directed (limited) our feedback with a checklist of criteria. We scored each criterion from one to ten, and that explained the final grade we awarded. This prevented unhelpful, unspecific criticism, such as informing the preacher that his first and only sermon attempt wasn't his best.

The *bēma* judgment is a detailed assessment of specific criteria we are warned about in the New Testament. Deeds, words, and motives are all appraised in the *bēma*, and they all affect our rewards.

Deeds

Christians rightly become a bit nervous when hearing teaching that ties deeds to rewards. The heroic saints of the Reformation toiled to clarify that salvation is by grace alone, through faith alone, apart from the works of the sinner. So we must approach this topic with caution. It is crucial to understand that the works believers do after salvation are in response to the grace we have received, motivated by love to God, and empowered entirely by the Holy Spirit, who works out God's will in our lives (Philippians 2:13). But a right understanding of these post-salvation deeds helps us to recognize the effect they have on our eternal rewards.

Note the way these passages, some of which we've seen already, assert that our deeds will be rewarded.

- "He will render to each one *according to his works*: to those who by patience in well-doing seek for glory and honor and immortality, he will give eternal life" (Romans 2:6-7). Here one's salvation is evidenced in commensurate deeds.

- "Now if anyone builds on the foundation with gold, silver, precious stones, wood, hay, straw—*each one's work* will become manifest, for the Day will disclose it, because it will be revealed by fire, and the fire will test *what sort of work each one has done.* If the work that anyone has built on the foundation survives, he will receive a reward. If anyone's work is burned up, *he will suffer loss, though he himself will be saved,* but only as through fire" (1 Corinthians 3:12-15).

- "For we must all appear before the judgment seat of Christ, so that each one may receive what is due for *what he has done in the body,* whether good or evil" (2 Corinthians 5:10).

- "Behold, I am coming soon, bringing my recompense with me, to *repay everyone for what he has done*" (Revelation 22:12).

There is no denying that the Scriptures indicate a correlation between works and rewards. But how are these verses compatible with our understanding of grace by faith alone, apart from our deeds? The apostle Paul, champion of grace by faith alone, masterfully explains the balance for us.

For by grace you have been saved through faith. And this is not your own doing; it is the gift of God, not a result of works, so that no one may boast. For we are his workmanship, created in Christ Jesus *for good works, which God prepared beforehand, that we should walk in them* (Ephesians 2:8-10).

What a gracious master we serve: He saves us, equips us, supplies us with work, empowers us to accomplish it, and then rewards us for that which we did in His strength!

Words

A particular subcategory of our deeds—our words—receives a special focus in Scripture. This is to be expected because words are a barometer of the conditions brewing in our hearts (Luke 6:45). For example, when the hypocritical Pharisees attributed Jesus' works to the devil, He lashed at them with righteous indignation.

> The good person out of his good treasure brings forth good,
> and the evil person out of his evil treasure brings forth evil.
> I tell you, on the day of judgment people will give account
> for every careless word they speak, for by your words you
> will be justified, and by your words you will be condemned
> (Matthew 12:35-37).

Though the recipients of this scolding were unbelievers, the insight that words will receive special attention on the judgment day should be sobering. And believers (specifically, Christian teachers) also receive a somber warning.

> Not many of you should become teachers, my brothers, for
> you know that we who teach will be judged with greater
> strictness. For we all stumble in many ways. And if anyone
> does not stumble in what he says, he is a perfect man, able
> also to bridle his whole body (James 3:1).

Imagine for a moment that a fastidious team of researchers was archiving every e-mail, text message, Tweet, or Facebook status update you have ever typed. Would that make you nervous? What if you discovered that a comprehensive compilation of your output—including transcripts of every conversation you've had and every sound you've mumbled under your breath—was to be printed and published as a book for the entire world to read? That would be quite a revealing (and voluminous) artifact, wouldn't it?

The Bible teaches that the Judge, who is to determine your reward, is keeping track of everything you say.

Motives

God not only hears everything you say and sees everything you do, He also knows everything you think, everything you feel, and everything you mean to say! As Jesus said, "Whatever you have said in the dark shall be heard in the light, and what you have whispered in private rooms shall be proclaimed on the housetops" (Luke 12:3).

Paul, too, acknowledged the scrutiny of motives in the judgment.

> I am not aware of anything against myself, but I am not thereby acquitted. It is the Lord who judges me. Therefore do not pronounce judgment before the time, before the Lord comes, who will bring to light the things now hidden in darkness and will *disclose the purposes of the heart*. Then each one will receive his commendation from God (1 Corinthians 4:4-5).

Two people may do the same deed but with very different motives. Anything done with impure motives—even that which appears praiseworthy—will be disregarded. Only that which is done to the glory of God will survive the judgment.

Faithfulness

God does not reward according to what you do, but rather according to what you do with what you have. No one is responsible to do more than what has been entrusted to him. As Jesus clearly warned, "Everyone to whom much was given, of him much will be required, and from him to whom they entrusted much, they will demand the more" (Luke 12:48).

As Helen Keller once said, "I long to accomplish some great and noble task, but I am to do small tasks as if they were great and noble." Some of us are more limited than others in the scope of our ministry. But thankfully, God rewards only our faithfulness to do the best with what we have.

Conclusion: Immunity Is Not Impunity

She never knew what hit her. The 16-year-old girl had recently moved with her mother to Washington, DC, where she attended school and easily made friends. They would soon attend her funeral.

She was out late. Just before midnight on the fateful night of Friday, January 3, 1997, as the car she was in casually approached DuPont Circle, the sound of shrieking tires, breaking glass, and buckling steel signaled a fleeting and chilling warning that probably barely registered in her awareness before…

The smoldering, five-car wreck claimed the girl's life and left four others seriously injured. The culprit was a drunk driver who had been bulleting through the city streets as if they were part of his own private Formula One playground. He plowed at full throttle into several cars stopped at a traffic light. He emerged unscathed and surrendered to the police with cavalier compliance, like a stroppy child who knows there will be no consequence for his naughtiness.

Sure enough, despite his obvious intoxication level and the corpse at the scene, the man was speedily released from custody. The police had no grip on this slippery character because of the license plate on his car.

As it turned out, the driver was a foreigner, the deputy ambassador of his country. According to the 1961 Vienna Convention on Diplomatic Relations, the envoys of the 187 signatory countries enjoyed immunity from prosecution in the countries in which they were serving.

But in a twist of satisfying justice, the criminal's immunity was waived by his superiors. A year later he was sentenced to serve seven to twenty-one years in prison for involuntary manslaughter.

The victim's mother eloquently summed up the outcome with a pithy flourish. "My daughter will not come back, but it has been worth the fight because immunity is not impunity."

Well said indeed. Immunity from the law does not mean impunity from all consequence, even in theological terms. We would be wrong to assume that because our sins are forgiven, we believers are not held accountable in this life or the next. The lesson we take from the *bēma* judgment is that immunity from condemnation is not impunity from consequence. May God enable us all to be faithful with His gifts, to use them for His glory, and then to enjoy His gracious rewards to the degree we were obedient.

////////////////////// **INSIGHTS FROM THE PAST** //////////////////////

Fellow servants giving account, and the whole world standing by that awful judgment-seat, and those who have lived from Adam unto His coming, having an account demanded of them of all that they did, how shall they but tremble, and be shaken?

John Chrysostom, Homily 76.3, as cited in Tim LaHaye and Thomas Ice, *The End Times Controversy* (Eugene, OR: Harvest House, 2003), 40

CHURCH DISCIPLINE

Taking the Fangs Out of It

MIKE ABENDROTH

Add the heightened imagination of a young boy to the observation deck of the La Brea Tar Pits, and what do you have? You have saber-toothed cats ferociously attacking mammoths mercilessly wedged in the tar. Blood everywhere. Shrieks. Snarls. Snorts. Savage *Smilodons* (the genus of the saber-tooth cat, and Greek for "chisel tooth") force-fully delivering their long canines deeply into the hide of their immov-able prey. These are the feral fantasies of most of the middle-school field-trip attendees. Conjure up a 1000-pound, rapacious attacker with 11-inch teeth. Chisels with a vengeance. Razor-sharp daggers on ste-roids. People who are frightened by grizzly bears have never envisaged a saber-toothed cat attacking a wooly mammoth.

I will never forget the day when I felt the spiritual equivalent of two canines perforating my trachea. As people recall where they were when President Kennedy was assassinated or when the space shuttle *Challenger* exploded, I remember exactly where I was the first time I heard a particular person's name read in church. It was not during the announcements, and it was not about a beach barbeque. It was not concerning a home-group get-together or a soup kitchen outreach event.

The pastor read the person's name and stated that the person was in unrepentant sin.

Gulp. It's hard to breathe with a saber-like tooth in your throat. Or a huge cat on your chest.

The pastor read the person's first name and last name from the pulpit. Slowly. With the microphone on. I was stunned. I'm surprised I didn't have to clear my throat, but it's hard to cough when a veritable *Smilodon* has you in its clutches.

Then the pastor read the following words from Jesus.

> If your brother sins against you, go and tell him his fault, between you and him alone. If he listens to you, you have gained your brother. But if he does not listen, take one or two others along with you, that every charge may be established by the evidence of two or three witnesses. If he refuses to listen to them, tell it to the church. And if he refuses to listen even to the church, let him be to you as a Gentile and a tax collector. Truly, I say to you, whatever you bind on earth shall be bound in heaven, and whatever you loose on earth shall be loosed in heaven. Again I say to you, if two of you agree on earth about anything they ask, it will be done for them by my Father in heaven. For where two or three are gathered in my name, there am I among them (Matthew 18:15-20).

And in my Bible, the words were in red. I could not get the refrain out of my mind. *Tell it to the church… Tell it to the church…* And my pastor did just that. He told it to the church. I was no longer flummoxed and mentally discombobulated. A man refused to deal with his sin, and the church did what the Lord Jesus said to do. I wanted to question the wisdom of the pastor, but the text was the text. My worldly influenced gut said, *The gall of the pastor!* But the Scriptures said, "Tell it to the church." The words from Scripture were as clear as could be.

Animals got lodged in the La Brea Tar Pits because a layer of water sat on top of the tar. The unsuspecting animals sauntered into the watering hole for some refreshment and maybe a bath. But once in the tar, there was no extraction until thousands of years later when scientists used mechanical cranes to do the job. Similarly, beneath the water of the world's wisdom and sagacity lies a tar-infested worldview.

We live in a litigious society. Here, the consumer is king or queen. Memberships in clubs and fraternal organizations are eroding, especially when members are required to do anything. Membership fees and dues are nearly as extinct as the mammoth or saber-toothed cat. The contemporary philosophy is simple: If you expect anything from your followers, they will leave. People like to coast. Float. Relax.

Yet the New Testament demands something from the followers of Jesus Christ. Consumerism, with its laziness and detachment, may be running amok in this age, but Scripture doesn't allow it in the church. Christ's "dues" are enormous. He requires all of you, not just a monthly membership fee you can pay online.

Church membership has its privileges in the person and work of Jesus Christ. It also has its expectations and demands, including personal holiness. When holiness is compromised, we can follow the clear biblical instructions. But beware. Even though a child can understand church discipline, only courageous men and women of God can enact what the Scriptures teach.

Let's survey each of the four steps of church discipline Jesus outlines in Matthew 18.

Step One

> If your brother sins against you, go and tell him his fault, between you and him alone. If he listens to you, you have gained your brother (verse 15).

Jesus does not endorse gossip or pleas to a "prayer chain" (I have always disliked chains of any kind). If a Christian is stuck in the rut of a particular sin, a church member who knows about the situation is to go to the offender and reveal his or her fault. To "tell him his fault" is to bring his situation to light, offer a scriptural point of view, and explain the reasoning behind it. As the Holy Spirit convicts the world concerning sin (John 16:8), so must the body of Christ convict a fellow Christian caught in sin. It must be done in private, and it must not be done for the reason of passing judgment or with the air of superiority.

Solomon's wisdom is very similar.

> Better is open rebuke
>   than hidden love.
> Faithful are the wounds of a friend;
>   profuse are the kisses of an enemy
> (Proverbs 27:5-6).

"If he listens to you…" We hope the guilty person responds to the loving confrontation by listening. To listen means much more than audibly perceiving a voice at a certain pitch and decibel level. Rather, it means to take in the information and heed it by obeying. If he repents, you have won your brother. As financial investors earn profit for their clients, so a courageous and humble Christian *gains* a brother when he goes to him in private and seeks his repentance. Upon repentance, the case is closed. It is not to be further mentioned. Period. Isn't that what you would want if you were caught in sin and then repented?

Here are some items to consider before you go to your sinning brother or sister.

- Have I prayed about the situation? Have I asked God for wisdom?
- Am I assuming the best?
- Am I going for God's glory?
- Am I going for the person's good (and not just to say, "Don't mess with me")?
- Is this a sin that should be covered?

If step one doesn't work…

Step Two

> But if he does not listen, take one or two others along with you, that every charge may be established by the evidence of two or three witnesses (Matthew 18:16).

Jesus echoes an Old Testament legal principle stemming from Deuteronomy 19:15: "A single witness shall not suffice against a person for any crime or for any wrong in connection with any offense that he has committed. Only on the evidence of two witnesses or of three witnesses shall a charge be established." Single witnesses could not righteously convict. Multiple witnesses were needed to establish credibility, ensure truth, and guarantee objectivity.

Both the confrontation and the sinner's response must be confirmed by multiple witnesses. Notice that the circle of people "in the know" is still extremely small. Gossip is avoided. Slander is forbidden. Pleading for repentance is mandatory.

Jesus does not tell us how much time should transpire between step one and step two, but we do know that if the person repents, we are to drop all charges and rejoice with the penitent.

If steps one and two don't work...

Step Three

> If he refuses to listen to them, tell it to the church (Matthew 18:17).

Step three is the step that normally throws people for a loop. The first two steps are done in private, and rightfully so. Why is the church told in this step? Answer: so the church family members can pray for their fallen comrade, beg for his repentance, and maintain their own healthy fear of sin. The news of the situation almost takes people's breath away, and that bears witness to the gravity and seriousness of the situation.

The church is told. Jesus did not instruct us to tell the elder board, the governing church body, the pope, or a group of bishops. Jesus does not instruct us to take it to the secular courts. He would not want the scoop posted on social media sites. Tell it to the church. They are the ones who live with or by the unrepentant member and are responsible to care for the person.

To tell only the Wednesday night prayer meeting group makes no sense. When a man on a ship goes overboard, all hands are called on deck for the rescue operation. Collective calls to repentance are ordered by the Lord, and when they are heeded, everything ceases except for the rejoicing.

If steps one, two, and three don't work...

Step Four

> And if he refuses to listen even to the church, let him be to
> you as a Gentile and a tax collector (Matthew 18:17).

Gulp. (Move Adam's apple slowly.) Step four has terrifying ramifications. One bad apple could spoil the whole bunch. Unrepentant sin is injurious to the whole congregation. Technically, Jesus wants the person excommunicated (literally, "out of community"). No more fellowship, Lord's Supper, or any other benefit the church offers. Step four is the equivalent to a heartbroken father stacking all his wayward son's clothes out on the sidewalk in front of the house. Gentiles were excluded from the old covenant, and in much the same manner, sinners who will not listen will be ostracized. For their own good. For the good of the church. For God's glory.

Paul tutors the Corinthians to follow through on step four.

> When you are assembled in the name of the Lord Jesus and
> my spirit is present, with the power of our Lord Jesus, you
> are to deliver this man to Satan for the destruction of the
> flesh, so that his spirit may be saved in the day of the Lord
> (1 Corinthians 5:4-5).

The ravaging of Satan just might drive the person back to the Lord in repentance. Scary.

Step four is not optional. Neither is this an isolated text—it is seen as a command elsewhere. "Now we command you, brothers, in the name of our Lord Jesus Christ, that you keep away from any brother who is walking in idleness and not in accord with the tradition that you received from us" (2 Thessalonians 3:6). Again, repentance instantly restores the person and the privileges of fellowshipping in the church of the Lord Jesus Christ.

Numbing the Pain

Online videos show veterinarians removing lions' and tigers' teeth for various reasons. The vets wisely anesthetize the beasts first! It's hard to smell things over the Internet, but the tawny animals look like they have bad breath. Let's look at seven questions that can take the edge off the frightening topic of church discipline. Think of the following discussion as scriptural lidocaine, which will numb the gum area before we extract any long fangs. "This shot isn't going to hurt too much. It will just be like a little bee sting."

Injection 1: Doesn't every society have rules and regulations?

Public schools with no rules? Homes with no curfews? Businesses with no protocols? Military service with no orders? It should come as no surprise that the church must obey commands and perform duties. Our society might want to reject authority in the abstract, but it still knows not to embrace anarchy. John Calvin agrees.

> But because some persons, in their hatred of discipline, recoil from its very name, let them understand this: if no society, indeed, no house which has even a small family, can be kept in proper condition without discipline, it is much more necessary in the church, whose condition should be as ordered as possible...Therefore, all who desire to remove discipline or to hinder its restoration, whether they do this deliberately or out of ignorance, are surely contributing to the ultimate dissolution of the church.[1]

Injection 2: The Lord Jesus purchased the church. Wouldn't He want to protect her purity?

Jesus Christ is the Lord and the head of the church. Therefore, the local church is to honor the King by obeying His edicts. The church is not a club, but a bride, and Jesus has paid a steep price for her. In Mark 10:45, Jesus describes the price He paid for His bride, the church. "For even the Son of Man came not to be served but to serve, and to give his life as a ransom for many." Jesus purchased the church with His own blood (Acts 20:28). He owns her. He wants a pure bride. He is concerned for the holiness of the church, and we should be too. A desire for a pure church should trump the fear of man, the possibility of lawsuits, pragmatism, and preference. If you do not like church discipline, you need to start with Jesus, not you. If the church were a human product to be marketed, then discipline could be debated. But Jesus calls the church, "my church" (Matthew 16:18).

Injection 3: What's love got to do with it?

The absence of church discipline is unloving. On multiple levels. Failure to obey God shows that we are not loving God, because those who love Him keep His commandments. John wrote, "And this is love, that we walk according to his commandments; this is the commandment, just as you have heard from the beginning, so that you should walk in it" (2 John 6).

Additionally, negligence in performing discipline shows that we are not loving the church. "Oh well, my body has treatable cancer, but I'm worried about what chemotherapy will do to my hairline." Sin in the body of Christ can affect other people. It's dangerous, but it's also correctable. So for the love of others, it must be dealt with according to the Bible. If you really hate other Christians, leave them totally alone when they get stuck. Love wants to reclaim offenders. Love for the lost sheep goes into the wilderness to restore them (see Luke 15). Loving God, loving the church, and loving the unrepentant sinner do not add up to a witch hunt in the church. Not going to the wayward person would actually be the most hateful thing you could do. Should you warn your neighbors when their house is on fire, or should you let them sleep through it?

The church that doesn't lovingly confront and correct its members is not being kind, forgiving, or gracious. Such a church is actually hindering the Lord's work and the advance of the gospel. A church without discipline is a church without purity (see Ephesians 5:25-27) and power (see Joshua 7:11-12). By neglecting church discipline, a church endangers not only its spiritual effectiveness but also its very existence. God snuffed out the candle of the church at Thyatira because of moral compromise (Revelation 2:20-24). Churches today are in danger of following this first-century precedent.[2] "Lack of church discipline is to be seen for what it really is—not a loving concern as is hypocritically claimed, but an indifference to the honor of Christ and the welfare of the flock." [3]

Injection 4: Don't we expect good human fathers to discipline?

> And have you forgotten the exhortation that addresses you as sons?
>> "My son, do not regard lightly the discipline of the Lord,
>>   nor be weary when reproved by him.
>> For the Lord disciplines the one he loves,
>>   and chastises every son whom he receives."
>
> It is for discipline that you have to endure. God is treating you as sons. For what son is there whom his father does not discipline? If you are left without discipline, in which all have participated, then you are illegitimate children and not sons. Besides this, we have had earthly fathers who disciplined us and we respected them. Shall we not much more be subject to the Father of spirits and live? For they disciplined us for a short time as it seemed best to them, but he disciplines us for our good, that we may share his holiness. For the moment all discipline seems painful rather than pleasant, but later it yields the peaceful fruit of righteousness to those who have been trained by it (Hebrews 12:5-11).
>
> Those whom I love, I reprove and discipline, so be zealous and repent (Revelation 3:19).

Injection 5: What should our attitude be if we have to confront others?

> Brothers, if anyone is caught in any transgression, you who are spiritual should restore him in a spirit of gentleness. Keep watch on yourself, lest you too be tempted. Bear one another's burdens, and so fulfill the law of Christ. For if anyone thinks he is something, when he is nothing, he

deceives himself. But let each one test his own work, and then his reason to boast will be in himself alone and not in his neighbor. For each will have to bear his own load (Galatians 6:1-5).

Injection 6: Does God ever use scare tactics?

Do not admit a charge against an elder except on the evidence of two or three witnesses. As for those who persist in sin, rebuke them in the presence of all, so that the rest may stand in fear (1 Timothy 5:19-20).

Injection 7: What has church history taught us?

The Reformation taught that a real church had three essential components: the preaching of the Word, the administration of the sacraments and ordinances, and church discipline.

The Belgic Confession (1561) listed three features "by which the true church is known." These marks are the preaching of pure doctrine, the administration of the sacraments, and the exercise of church discipline. The Heidelberg Catechism makes a bold statement: "Question 83. What are the keys of the kingdom of heaven? Answer: The preaching of the holy gospel, and Christian discipline, or excommunication out of the Christian church; by these two, the kingdom of heaven is opened to believers, and shut against unbelievers."

The biblical concept of church discipline is so simple that even children can understand it. Children could teach the concept. But beware—the Bible's instruction for discipline is so difficult to perform that only Holy Spirit–energized elders and congregations will be able to institute it. This is not the return of the scarlet letter, but neither is it for the faint of heart.

Practical Helps for the Local Church

1. Include church discipline practices in your church bylaws. Publish them online too.

2. Require all new membership classes to teach church discipline.

3. Remember your own sinfulness before confronting someone who has fallen.

4. Be involved in the lives of other Christians.

5. Support your pastors and elders when steps 3 and 4 are executed.

6. If your church does not teach church discipline as Jesus describes in Matthew 18, make an appointment to talk to your pastors or church leaders about it.

Conclusion

Church discipline is not macabre. It is mandatory. Did you know that the term "saber-toothed tiger" is actually a misnomer? There is no such animal. As a species, saber-toothed cats are not related to tigers. So why did we all grow up saying "saber-toothed tiger"? Similarly, why did most of us grow up in churches where discipline was extinct? "Saber-toothed tiger" is misleading, and so is a church that has no desire for purity and discipline.

Maybe scarlet letters should be attached to the buildings of churches that *don't* practice church discipline.

INSIGHTS FROM THE PAST

Westminster Confession of Faith (1646)
Of Church Censures

III. Church censures are necessary, for the reclaiming and gaining of offending brethren, for deterring of others from the like offenses, for purging out of that leaven which might infect the whole lump, for vindicating the honor of Christ, and the holy profession of the Gospel, and for preventing the wrath of God, which might justly fall upon the Church, if they should suffer His covenant, and the seals thereof, to be profaned by notorious and obstinate offenders.

IV. For the better attaining of these ends, the officers of the Church are to proceed by admonition; suspension from the sacrament of the Lord's Supper for a season; and by excommunication from the Church; according to the nature of the crime, and demerit of the person.

13

ELDER RULE

Big Brother or an Orwellian Nightmare?

CLINT ARCHER

George Orwell's seminal political satire *Nineteen Eighty-Four* portrays a nightmarish state that is inescapably oppressed by a totalitarian government. Every minute aspect of this dystopian society is monitored and governed by the unopposed and tyrannical Party. The dictator who leads the Party is a quasi-divine figurehead known as Big Brother. Information about citizens is gathered by seemingly omnipresent surveillance technology, and fear is instilled through ubiquitous propaganda posters with the ominous slogan, "Big Brother is watching you."

The idea that there is someone assigned to watch over you can be quite unsettling. People don't want to be looked after. We see it as patronizing, like hiring a babysitter for a teenager. Or it's downright creepy, as if you discovered a stalker's collection of photographs of you.

But from a different perspective, having someone watch over you can be comforting. The victim of a schoolyard bully would feel reassured if his older brother promised, "I'll be watching over you this week at recess. No one will hurt you on my watch." Likewise, the president is probably relieved to know that while his eyes are closed in public prayer, his bodyguards are perpetually vigilant and attentive to the slightest threat of danger. A country can get on with its business knowing that there is a strong and prepared military that is constantly analyzing intelligence and monitoring potential threats to the safety of its citizenry.

The thought of church government and elders may bring you fear or comfort. Which of those reactions you have is probably determined by your experience. You may have witnessed the wise and godly use of authority, or perhaps you were burned by the sinful abuse of church leadership. Your understanding of the New Testament pattern for church leaders will also influence your attitude. Exposure to poor leadership in a church is one of the most frequent excuses professing believers offer for not attending church. Conversely, the healthiest churches are those with good leadership.

Ultimately, we need to come to terms with what the Bible says about elders. God knows what is best for His flock. He outlines the qualifications for elders, He supplies their job description, He limits their authority, and He alone prescribes their role and function in the church.

Title Fight: The Biblical Terms

Pastors use business cards as an efficient way of transmitting contact details. But the card can also be a barometer of a church's view of biblical leadership. If the pastor's card says Regional Bishop of the Eastern District, you can surmise his denomination has a rigid, geographically based hierarchy. If his name is precede by The Right Reverend Most Holy Apostle, you likewise have an idea of the view his church has of its leaders (or at least the view he wants them to have). Some titles are intended to convey the church's position on issues. If you're having lunch with an Anointed Prophet and High Priest of the Flaming Old Covenant Tabernacle Ministries, you might want to avoid recommending the pulled pork sandwich.

Some churches create leadership offices ex nihilo for whatever new ministry programs they concoct. Their office doors have nameplates with titles like "Pastor of Media Outreach," "Chairman of Angelic Visitations," and "Associate Pastor of Light and Sound Therapy." What a long way we have come since the Reformers decided to ditch the High-Church appellation *priest* for the humble designation *pastor*, which simply means shepherd. These days, *pastor* can be misused as a title of honor and respect. Ministers go by Reverend or even Doctor if they have studied enough. Some pursue postgraduate degrees simply to add the coveted *Dr.* to their business card. The spiritual leaders of Israel felt this way.

> They love…greetings in the marketplaces and being called rabbi by others. But you are not to be called rabbi, for you have one teacher, and you are all brothers. And call no man your father on earth, for you have one Father, who is in heaven. Neither be called instructors, for you have one instructor, the Christ. The greatest among you shall be your servant (Matthew 23:7-11).

The New Testament titles for church leaders show us how we should view them and how they should view themselves. The New Testament employs three primary terms to describe spiritual leaders in the church. Each holds insights into the function and position of the servant-leaders of a healthy church.

At the Helm: Elders Are Leaders

The term *elder* (Greek, *presbuteros*, as used in Acts 14:23; 1 Timothy 5:17; 1 Peter 5:1) refers to a person's seniority and maturity. Some churches use the English term *presbyter* to refer to their leaders; that usage stems from this word. The word does not necessarily imply an advanced age, for Paul reminded the youthful elder Timothy, "Let no one despise you for your youth" (1 Timothy 4:12). But maturity, both emotionally and spiritually, is an essential quality of the elder. Paul stipulated as much in his list of qualifications for elders: "He must not be a recent convert, or he may become puffed up with conceit and fall into the condemnation of the devil" (1 Timothy 3:6).

The need for seniority is simply that someone needs to lead. Jesus chose 12 men to lead the early church. Among them he instituted informal tiers. Peter, James, and John (and occasionally Andrew) were the inner circle. They were leaders among leaders, exposed to privileged times of instruction and observation (see Matthew 17:1; Mark

5:37; 13:3; 14:33). And even among this core group, Peter emerged as the first among equals. In every list of the 12, Peter is always mentioned first, and he functioned as the spokesman time and again. Jesus singles Peter out as the rock on which the church will be built (Matthew 16:18) and leaves the care of the disciples in his hands (John 21:15).

This is not to say Peter, or the inner circle, or any leaders in the church are superheroes of spirituality. History is replete with the failings of those in leadership. But God calls elders to their role and equips them with spiritual gifts. Paul describes the leaders themselves as gifts of God to the church (Ephesians 4:11).

A seminary professor of mine often reminded his students neither to be puffed up by position nor to feel inadequate for the task ahead. He used this pithy metaphor to remind us that we were feeble leaders equipped by God's grace to impart something of value to our churches: "In the country of blind men, the one-eyed is king." Human leaders are indeed weak creatures, but by God's calling and equipping, they have a responsibility to lead the flock. In this sense they are elders, or seniors, manning the helm and steering the church according to the bearing God has set in His Word.

Men of the (Wash)Cloth: Elders Are Servant-Leaders

The word *overseer* (Greek, *episkopos*, as used, for example, in Philippians 1:1; 1 Timothy 3:2; and Titus 1:5) means one who gives oversight or has authority over a group or situation as a watchman or superintendent. As the meaning suggests, the leaders of a church are there to provide spiritual oversight and authority. This is why the writer of Hebrews tells church members, "Obey your leaders and submit to them, for they are keeping watch over your souls" (Hebrews 13:17). The Greek word translated "keeping watch" in this verse means "to abstain from sleep, to keep awake." Church leaders are never to fall asleep at the wheel or doze off on duty, but are to keep watch to protect and guide the flock God has entrusted to them.

Jesus explained that spiritual authority in the church is not like secular authority in the world.

You know that the rulers of the Gentiles lord it over them, and their great ones exercise authority over them. It shall not be so among you. But whoever would be great among you must be your servant, and whoever would be first among you must be your slave, even as the Son of Man came not to be served but to serve, and to give his life as a ransom for many (Matthew 20:25-28).

Jesus repeatedly taught and modeled that leaders in His church are to be servants of the flock. He donned a slave's towel and stooped to wash His disciples' reeking feet to prove that men of the cloth are to be men of the washcloth!

Fencing the Flock: Elders Are Bodyguards

The English word *pastor* is spelled the same as the Latin word for a herdsman, or shepherd. The Greek word *poimēn* is used in 1 Peter 5:1 as a verb—"shepherd the flock"—and refers to the work the leaders do. The shepherd is an apt metaphor for spiritual oversight, one that Jesus used of Himself, because the job description has many parallels with church work.

Shepherds feed their sheep just as pastors nourish their congregation with teaching from God's Word (2 Timothy 3:16-17). Pastors guide the church in making decisions by directing them to the Scriptures, rebuking them when they sin, and exhorting them to obey God (2 Timothy 4:2), just as shepherds guide their sheep to safe and healthy pastures.

Shepherds are also guardians. The body of Christ needs to be guarded from the assault of error. Our fight is not a struggle against flesh and blood, but a spiritual warfare (Ephesians 6), so our bodyguards need to be men of spiritual stature and confidence. Guarding the flock from predators was a shepherd's responsibility, just as a pastor is tasked with defending the faith and exposing false teachers, who would spread dangerous doctrines and ravage the church like wolves (Acts 20:28-30).

This is noble work indeed. But before the pastor prints a new batch of business cards and embosses auspicious words like "Guardian and Guide" on them, let's not forget that the title is not one to be flaunted. People who tended sheep were considered to be unsophisticated, uncouth, and socially undesirable. Theirs was not a position to be proud of. The work was extremely important but nonetheless a dirty job that someone had to stoop to do. This is how Jesus wants His under-shepherds to view their position: "Shepherd the flock of God that is among you...not domineering over those in your charge, but being examples to the flock. And when the chief Shepherd appears, you will receive the unfading crown of glory" (1 Peter 5:2-4).

The pastor's reward for faithfulness will come in heaven, not in the marketplace.

Walk This Way: Elders Are Examples

Elders don't just teach the Word; they model it. Their lives are motion pictures of what Jesus' teachings should look like in practice. The flock will follow the leaders on the path of sanctification, even attempting to mimic the way they walk and match their pace. This is why Peter instructed pastors to lead in humility.

Power in the Pulpit: Elders Are Teachers

One of the elder's primary roles is that of teacher (1 Timothy 3:1-2). The New Testament is unambiguous about the need for pastors to preach, teach, exhort, rebuke, counsel, admonish, encourage, and otherwise dispense truth (see 1 Thessalonians 5:14; 2 Timothy 4:2).

Not all elders will carry the same weight of a church's teaching load, but the primacy of this role is seen, for example, in Paul's instruction on remuneration of full-time preachers. "Let the elders who rule well be considered worthy of double honor, especially those who labor in preaching and teaching" (1 Timothy 5:17).

Making the Grade

In many martial arts, grading is awarded on the basis of two seemingly unrelated criteria—competence and character. One understands the need for a demonstration of competence. If a martial artist cannot perform the requisite katas and display his or her proficiency, then failure can be expected. But in many dojos, fancy kicks and airborne swirls are not enough to garner the coveted black belt. The student must also show self-control, respect, and discipline. No matter how many blocks of wood you can chop through bare-handed or how dexterously you master your opponent in sparring bouts, if you show disrespect to your opponent or the grading council, or if you behave in an unsportsmanlike manner, the verdict will not be favorable.

In the church, more so than in any other arena of life, the character of a person is as integral to leadership positions as is competence. In fact, only two abilities are required for an elder in the church. The bulk of the requirements have to do with one's character. Paul gave Timothy a list of qualifications to use as criteria when appointing elders in the fledgling churches around Ephesus. These lists should be the sole source of criteria for churches appointing elders. A person may be influential in the community, he might have acquired impressive wealth or academic credentials, or he could be a really nice guy, but these laurels can wilt with time and pressure. God's standards are much more telling and necessary for the work He calls elders to perform.

Competence

Job interviewers often ask applicants what they consider to be their strengths and weaknesses. One tactic is to list weaknesses that the boss would consider strengths. "Oh, my weakness is that I am a perfectionistic workaholic, which is why I make my job my whole life." Another slightly more honest strategy is to admit your weakness in a way that emphasizes a strength. "I'm new to this industry, but I make up for inexperience by being a quick learner and hard worker."

But a savvy human resources interviewer needs to know whether you can actually do the job for which you are applying. A chemical plant needs a chemical engineer with a degree more than it needs perfectionistic workaholics. No amount of personality and character will make up for the lack of basic required abilities. And yet many churches appoint their leaders based on how likeable they are and how enthusiastically they are involved in church events. Elders don't need a vast array of superpowers, but they do need to have at least these two fundamental skills: the abilities to teach and to lead.

The most important skill an elder needs to possess is the ability to teach (1 Timothy 3:2). This makes perfect sense, as his function in the church is to teach the Word (through preaching, conducting Bible studies, or counseling people), to defend the faith against false teachers, and to guide the flock to make wise decisions as laid out in the Bible. The ability to teach implies a thorough knowledge of the Scriptures and theology and skill at applying doctrines to everyday situations. Not all elders are good at preaching, but they all need to be able to know what the Bible says about a situation and then help people to apply that knowledge.

An elder must also be able to "manage his own household well, with all dignity keeping his children submissive" (1 Timothy 3:4). The management of a household covers many facets of oversight. To provide for a household involves financial planning (making a budget and sticking to it), delegation of responsibilities (chores), maintenance of facilities (such as mowing the lawn and paying the rent), concern for spiritual development (family worship times), teaching (from tying shoelaces to persevering at calculus), counseling (attending to broken hearts and dearly departed hamsters), and countless ways of serving. (Yes, carting kids to and from soccer practice counts as selfless service!)

Paul makes the point that family management is a good test of a person's competence for spiritual leadership. "For if someone does not know how to manage his own household, how will he care for God's church?" (1 Timothy 3:5).

Since the elders' task is to provide spiritual, financial, and strategic oversight for the church, it seems reasonable to expect them to have some evidence of their ability. What better way to assess the man's oversight skills than by watching the way he manages his family? A man's wife and children know him best. Do they respect him? Do they trust his judgment? Do they exhibit the type of fruit one would expect to see in a family where a godly and loving husband and father has been leading? These probing questions are worth pondering before appointing a man to an office that requires him to do for a large group of people essentially what God requires him to do for his own family: lead, teach, protect, rebuke, encourage, and serve.

This does not mean that a man must have perfect children or a well-bred litter of flawless spiritual pedigree. Children have minds of their own (though some use it more consistently than others). A father is not on trial for every misstep his children take over the years. The question is, how has he managed the issues of life that crop up? A church will present the same challenges we see in families—personal conflict, financial pressure, health trials—and the elder's response to these situations should prove consistent in wisdom and poise.

Character

Much of the paranoia about Orwellian dictators lording it over the church can be dispelled by the list of character traits that qualify one to be an elder. It's hard to imagine a totalitarian leader described in Paul's terms: "An overseer must be above reproach, the husband of one wife, sober-minded, self-controlled, respectable, hospitable, able to teach, not a drunkard, not violent but gentle, not quarrelsome, not a lover of money" (1 Timothy 3:2-3). These qualities are mandatory for overseers.

If the commitment to these qualities ebbs over time, the elder forfeits the right to continue in his office. Elders are disqualified when any of the required traits or abilities lapse. For example, if an elder changes his doctrine from what the church believes, he is no longer "able to teach." Or if he commits adultery, he is no longer a one-woman man. In either case, he should no longer be allowed to serve as an overseer.

When we hear horror stories of churches under the thumb of megalomaniac pastors and their gestapo elders, the biblical standards have not been applied. The solution is not to invent an unbiblical system to replace the biblical one. The solution is to implement the biblical system properly. Elders are not untouchable. They are even more strictly accountable to God's standards (James 3:1).

A natural concern arises at this point. What if the elder is disqualified (lacking in the necessary character) or just unqualified (lacking in the necessary abilities) and yet refuses to resign from the office? Good question, bad situation. Ungodly elders can infect the body of Christ.

They must be removed with urgency before their influence spreads like gangrene. Thankfully, God's Word supplies a potent remedy to that infection.

Dishonorable Discharge: What to Do About Bad Elders?

Elders will sin. They are human. As with any believer, the issue is, how do they respond when confronted with their sin? If repentance ensues, "you have gained your brother" (Matthew 18:15). If the elder repents and reforms his ways, then he is exemplifying what he should be teaching the flock. For example, suppose he told a lewd joke to a congregant who pointed out that this kind of off-color humor is unbecoming of one who is to be respectable and above reproach. The elder should humbly confess his sin, ask forgiveness, and then commit to stop his coarse jesting. This response shows maturity, humility, and godliness.

In other cases, however, the sin may require him to step down from the office of elder even if he is repentant. For example, an elder caught in adultery may confess and repent speedily, but he has still shown that he can no longer be characterized as a one-woman man. In this case, he should graciously resign so that the other elders aren't forced to remove him from office.

The problem comes when he persists in sin (1 Timothy 5:20). For instance, the elder might deny his sin or rationalize that it wasn't sin, or he may simply refuse to stop committing the sin. In this case the other elders must deal with that situation decisively and publicly. "Do not admit a charge against an elder except on the evidence of two or three witnesses. As for those who persist in sin, rebuke them in the presence of all, so that the rest may stand in fear" (1 Timothy 5:19-20).

The public rebuke will undo the sin's influence in the church. People may have been thinking, "Outbursts of anger are evidently acceptable behaviors for a believer because that elder is always erupting at church meetings." The public rebuke shows the congregation that the elders are serious about their own sin and will therefore be serious about the sin of anyone else in the church as well.

Requiring two or three witnesses prevents disgruntled individuals from accusing the elder with a fictitious charge. If multiple people have detected the same pattern in an elder and have brought these concerns to light, the other elders should address the pattern of behavior.

Conclusion: Who's Afraid of Their Big Brothers?

As freaky as it is to know someone is watching over you, the Bible portrays this reality as a blessed privilege of a healthy church. Elders are our big brothers—not the dictatorial Orwellian type, but the reassuring protective kind. These men spend their time in prayer for the flock, they labor to teach, they study diligently to guide, and they preach boldly to protect.

Paul wrote his young converts, "We ask you, brothers, to respect those who labor among you and are over you in the Lord and admonish you, and to esteem them very highly in love because of their work" (1 Thessalonians 5:12-13). We should not resent their involvement in our spiritual lives, but should cherish their care and cooperate with them. When parents leave an older brother in charge of the young ones, he is accountable to be responsible for his siblings, and they are expected to respect their parents' delegated authority.

As the writer of Hebrews says, "Obey your leaders and submit to them, for they are keeping watch over your souls, as those who will have to give an account. Let them do this with joy and not with groaning, for that would be of no advantage to you" (Hebrews 13:17). To a mature believer, this blessing is a cause for reassurance and comfort, not fear and suspicion.

///////////////////////// INSIGHTS FROM THE PAST /////////////////////////

The importance and necessity of a bishopric for each church, embodying gifts for various services, is thus most obvious for the accomplishment of one of the great ends for which Christ came into the world, and for which, when he ascended up on high, he received gifts for men. This end is stated at large in the following passage from the epistle to the Ephesian church: "For the perfecting of the saints, for the work of the ministry, for the edifying of the body of Christ; till we all come in the unity of the faith, and of the knowledge of the Son of God, unto a perfect man, unto the measure of the stature of the fulness of Christ; that we henceforth be no more children, tossed to and fro, and carried about with every wind of doctrine, by the sleight of men, and cunning craftiness, whereby they lie in wait to deceive; but speaking the truth in love, may grow up into him in all things, which is the Head, even Christ; from whom the whole body fitly joined together, and compacted by that which every joint supplieth, according to the effectual working in the measure of every part, maketh increase of the body unto the edifying of itself in love." Eph. iv: 12-16. This is the noble end for which "apostles, prophets, evangelists, pastors and teachers were given." A plurality in the bishopric is of great importance for mutual counsel and aid, that the government and edification of the flock may be promoted in the best manner. At stated meetings of the bishopric, the members would report their separate doings, and confer together upon the teachings of scripture, which they would bring forth to the church for its consideration and adoption. Such a body would constitute the proper council of advisers to the church collectively, and to the members individually. Interchangeably each would aid the other in his department, and when necessary, would unite in any one department. Oh, what a blessing would such a bishopric be to a church! But ah! Where are we to find men whose gifts fit them for composing such a bishopric? The answer is given in the passage above referred to. "When he ascended up on high, he led captivity captive, and gave gifts unto men—some apostles, some prophets, some evangelists, some pastors and teachers." To the ascended Redeemer and Head of the churches, must we go for these gifts. For he will be enquired of for them. The churches must desire them. They must understand this part of their divinely instituted order, and must earnestly wrestle with their Lord for the gifts that are necessary to carry it out.

W.B. Johnson, "The Rulers of the Church of Christ" in *The Gospel Developed Through the Government and Order of the Churches of Jesus Christ* (1846), as cited in Mark Dever, *Polity* (Washington, DC: Center for Church Reform, 2001), 193-94

14

HOMOSEXUALITY

Turns Out We Were All Born "This Way"

BYRON YAWN

We stopped at an Arby's outside Chattanooga on our way back to Nashville. An emaciated figure named Jim sat across from me, weeping into his meal. I had never seen a human being so totally broken. Pieces of him were strewn all over his life. He was reminiscent of those ubiquitous gaunt figures in Nazi concentration camps staring out from eyes that seemed too large for their sockets. His childhood friend and cousin, Tom, sat beside him, holding him up as he ate. We were quite the trio. I had met Jim just a half hour before.

Earlier in the day Tom called me with a vague description of a cousin who'd gotten himself in serious trouble. He needed help getting him out of it. I dropped what I was doing, walked out of my office, and sat in the passenger seat of Tom's car around noon. Where I'm from, you can assume what "trouble" means—methamphetamines or similar types of Southern delinquency. On the ride down I got the backstory. It was not what I was expecting.

Jim was 45. He was a lifelong practicing homosexual who was HIV positive. He had a legal union from Vermont with a partner of ten years. The two of them were living in Atlanta. Through a series of events, their relationship had turned violently out of control. After beating Jim and attacking him with a knife, the partner had bound and gagged him, leaving him to die in the back room of their suburban home. After days of captivity with no food or water, Jim struggled loose and climbed out a bedroom window while his partner was at work.

The only person he knew to turn to was Tom. Tom immediately called a ministry in Atlanta that serves the homosexual community. Then he called me. Four hours later the three of us were sitting in an Arby's.

No wonder Tom waited on the ride down to share the specifics.

Watching Tom put his arm around this diseased man startled me. To say I was uncomfortable being this close to a homosexual is an understatement. As a Southern conservative, I had been raised to stay away from gays. To hate them. I can remember taunting the few I knew of in my high school. I did it under the guise of righteous indignation. My brand of church and theology over the years had reinforced the idea that homosexuality was an especially heinous sin that incurred a peculiarly intense form of God's wrath. Any society that tolerated homosexuality was certain to incur His judgment. They are, after all, what's wrong with America. I had the biblical passages to prove it.

But that's not how I felt. I found myself caught between grace and truth.

My Pathetic Hateful Heart

We sat there in silence except for Jim's uncontrolled sobbing. Tom and I were witnessing that rare moment when a person reaches the end of himself. Not many of us ever do. Every few seconds, he heaved his shoulders upward, took in a desperate mouthful of air, and collapsed back down in a bend. It was a wheezy rhythm of brokenness.

Unexpectedly, from a place deep inside my heart, I caught the rhythm. I began to weep along with him. Partly for him but mainly for me. He was pathetic, but he was not as pathetic as me. My abominable hatred for another human being was thrown back at my feet. My self-righteous nose that allowed me to consider his sin more offensive than mine was being rubbed in the gospel of grace. His humanity and need for mercy was doing a number on my sanctified homophobia. I reached out, took his hand, and broke with generations of cruelty.

We were the same desperate leper bowed at the feet of the same Savior. Unclean. The untouchables.

I began talking. Fifteen minutes later I had dug underneath all the muck of his life and touched on the taproot of his current pain—sin and a need for forgiveness. Previously, Jim and I would have agreed that he was beyond God's forgiveness. Fixed in his rejection. But at this table, at this moment, Jim was the last remaining proponent of this conviction. "Where sin abounds, grace much more abounds." I laid out the gospel of God's grace with compassion and clarity. I set before him the righteousness that was not his own, but could be his by faith in the life, death, burial, and resurrection of Jesus Christ. He could be made clean this very day by faith.

I knew this lifestyle that lay on the surface was only a symptom of the same destructive idolatry running through every human heart. My heart. Strangely, at no point did I call him to repent of his homosexuality. I didn't need to, just as I don't tell a drunk guy he needs to flee his drunkenness. He knows this. Besides, drunkenness is not the reason he needs to flee to the mercy of God. Jesus did not die to help people sober up. The sequence of grace is not "clean yourself up and God will accept you," but "God accepts you—go and sin no more." Our nature is the problem. Someone outside of us has to touch our eyes and heal our blindness, touch our lives and raise us from the dead.

The gospel I preached that evening might well have been offered to a homeschooler. The same gospel applies to each equally. For when we speak in terms of the unapproachable purity of a holy God, there is no difference between a homeschooler and a homosexual among fallen men. "For all have fallen short." When I was done, he looked up at me with a thank-you on his face, and then looked back down. There was no reply.

We drove back in silence. Jim slept the entire way, no doubt having been exhausted for decades. When we arrived back in town, Tom took Jim into his own home with his wife and two young children. Tom's unswerving mercy toward this man was a rebuke to me. I'm certain I would not have done the same—family or not. We parted ways. I went home and shared the day's events with my wife.

I See It. It Is Glorious.

Two days later, while sitting in my office, I got another phone call. This time from Jim. "Byron. My eyes were opened. I see it. I see what you were talking about. God's grace is astounding. God has forgiven me of my sins. I'm free. Thank you for sharing the gospel with me. Thanks for coming to get me."

I wept again. Partly for Jim. Partly for me. I had so discounted the power of the gospel. Deep down I wondered to myself whether a person like Jim could actually be transformed by it. But indeed it does reach down that far. Quietly, on that very morning, while he was eating a bowl of cold cereal in Tom's kitchen, the light dawned in his heart. Jim called Tom. Then he called me.

Months later Jim stood before our congregation in the waters of baptism (we baptized him last so as not to scare to death the decent suburbanites who were baptized before him). He told the entire story. People sat stunned. He was baptized in the name of the Father and the Son and the Holy Spirit. Afterward a line formed at the front of the sanctuary as all of us who had spent our lives staying away from the likes of Jim embraced him. We needed to embrace him. Octogenarians. Middle-aged couples. Single adolescent males. Southerners. Moms. Families. Conservatives. This may have been as close as any of us had ever been to sheer grace. Jim had single-handedly altered our perception of gay people.

A few weeks later, as he was departing to live with family out of state, Jim addressed our church family for the last time. "You know that person you finally stopped praying for because he or she is too far gone? That individual you gave up on? I'm that person. Don't stop praying that God's grace would break through. It can raise the deadest sinner from the dead."

Overrun by Reality

Mainline and traditional churches have no idea what to do with the LGBT community or the debate underway in this country. We've spent so much time keeping ourselves from "those people," we've no idea what to do now that we can't. Our naïveté has been overrun by reality. Homosexuality has become mainstream. And this long ago. Same-sex relationships are largely acceptable in the popular culture. Within the church, various denominations specialize in accommodating a homosexual population. Others ordain homosexuals as clergy. Certain branches of the gay community are militantly pressing for popular acceptance of the homosexual lifestyle. Consequently, Christian convictions regarding morality and family values are lying in the middle of the political and cultural tracks. In some instances, to stand in opposition to the lifestyle (or to merely disagree with it) gets you branded as a hatemonger. You become an ex officio member of Westboro Baptist Church. The pressure on Christians is intense.

But before we puff up with righteous indignation against "the gay campaign of cultural conditioning" and take to the polls against such blatant opposition to Christian morals, we should know that extremist Christian groups have matched gay activism with raw hatred. Westboro Baptist Church of Topeka, Kansas, is the chief example. Their slogan is "God hates fags." Members of Westboro protest the funerals of American soldiers, condemning them and attributing their death to America's tolerance of the gay community. Most reasonable evangelicals find this sort of hate intolerable. But these same evangelicals are so repulsed by the gay lifestyle that they regularly justify their disdain for an entire demographic of people. The hypocrisy is patent.

Like so many issues in conservative evangelicalism, homosexuality is a place where we've confused our American family values with Christianity. These are not the same. We have been conditioned to confuse them. But wherever they may overlap, we must strive keep them distinct. Otherwise we will confuse the true mission of the church with cultural modification, whether it is the old fundamentalist version of moral reform or a more modern and delicate version of cultural transformation, such as "win the city."

Without losing sight of compassion, we must remember that our goal as Christians is not to craft an acceptable message for popular culture. That would be impossible because the cross is "foolishness." At the same time, our ultimate goal as Christians is not protecting the American way of life or defending conservative values. This too is impossible.

Doubtless, our politics and values will be informed by Christianity, but our politics and values are not Christianity.

Therefore, our mission as a church is not to protect the American way of life from the "gay agenda." People may choose to take up this cause, but they should not suppose they are thereby fulfilling their Christian duty. When a sermon on homosexuality in a conservative church morphs into activism and a diatribe on the decline of values in America, we're confusing one (American) with the other (Christian). On the other hand, when our dialogue with the gay community forbids the biblical perspective toward the lifestyle (sin), it is less about reasoned compassion and more about political correctness. Our mission as a church is to declare the gospel of Christ to individuals, whomever they may be and whatever consequence that may bring to their way of life.

> Then Jesus told his disciples, "If anyone would come after me, let him deny himself and take up his cross and follow me. For whoever would save his life will lose it, but whoever loses his life for my sake will find it. For what will it profit a man if he gains the whole world and forfeits his life? Or what shall a man give in return for his life?" (Matthew 16:24-26).

Some supposedly Christian attitudes toward the gay community have more in common with conservative Islam than with Christ. Historically, the church has lacked grace and compassion in this area. We have our favorite sins, and homosexuality is at the top of the list. Cheating on your taxes or hating entire groups of people in our communities remain low among our prioritized lists of sin. We've demonstrated no capacity or desire to minister to gay people. The idea that we are called to love them (not in word only but in deed as well) is repulsive to many. We've made this obvious, and they have received this message loud and clear.

Understandably, they are responding in kind. As I write this, pastors are suffering the consequences of the church's graceless vitriol. I don't mean pastors are being persecuted for merely holding a biblical view (which would be commendable), but that pastors are held in suspicion for the church's rather merciless treatment of gay people. Many high-profile evangelicals who have attempted to reach out are automatically blacklisted for stating the Bible's perspective. Many other notable evangelicals are distancing themselves from the church's traditional message on the subject. Still others are reconsidering our traditional approach altogether. We're beginning to discover that we've confused American with Christian.

Conservatives in this country—inside and outside the church—are quickly becoming the minority on this issue. The legality of same-sex unions and equal rights for gays are firmly embedded in the political debate. Christians and social conservatives in America appear to be on the wrong side of history. Eventually, we will lose this contest. The issue of homosexuality is here to stay. The question is, how is the church going to respond after losing the cultural debate? How should we respond to this community we've largely denied existed and mainly mistreated? These are important and unavoidable questions. Regardless of whether we condone the lifestyle, we've no option but to determine how Christ would have us respond.

And how should the church react to its own members who identify with this culture and lifestyle? This corner is hard to turn, but we must wake up to the notion that homosexuality is now present in our churches. Some may find this idea unacceptable, but if we doubt this, we're simply ignoring reality. It is in our churches. This is not to say that gay couples are sitting together in our membership classes or openly participating in our ministries. (Although they may be.) But at the very least, men and women who attend our churches silently struggle with their sexual identity, have engaged in homosexual activity on some level, or are related to or acquainted with someone who has. This includes born-again Christians. Some congregations may rarely encounter it, but that may be due simply to a fear of rejection. Fact is, if you were going to ask for help, the last place you would want to turn is the typical Christian church. Tragic.

The Intersection of Grace and Truth

The church and Christians seem to fall off on one of two sides of this issue without any real ability for balance. We're either so politically correct that we're afraid of calling homosexuality a sin, or we're so venomous in our disdain for the gay lifestyle that there's no sign of grace. We seem incapable of reconciling grace and truth. We're either cowardly and truthless or mean-spirited and graceless. In the minds of some, you betray the love of Christ if you call homosexuals to repentance. In the minds of others, you betray the truth if you show any understanding and compassion. Neither is correct. Ultimately, it is better to lay our biblical cards on the table and prove ourselves loving over time than to hide our cards through clever apologetics in an effort to be loved.

For the sake of discussion, I'll step in the trap of popular opinion by stating the biblical position. Homosexuality is a sin. I realize this is extremely offensive on a popular level, but the Bible makes this clear. Unless you warp the words of Scripture, which many do, you can hardly deny that this is what God says. God calls it an abomination. "You shall not lie with a male as with a woman; it is an abomination" (Leviticus 18:22). I also realize that terminology is old and bothersome, but you should know the Christian opinion gets worse. Christians believe that all mankind is destined for hell. And that without the intervention of God's grace, repentance from sin, and belief in the righteous substitutionary offering of the Son of God, no one will escape it. Not even social conservatives. Each of us is an abomination.

God hates all sin. (He put His Son to death as a result of it.) In fact, all sex outside of marriage (between a woman and man) is sinful. Regardless of what many decent church folk may think, homosexuality is not the only behavior God despises. Homosexuality is not what's wrong with this country. God will punish every unrepentant sinner and judge all sin, either through the cross or in the sinner himself. Self-righteous Christians seem to forget that God's hatred for sin includes some of our more acceptable white-collar heterosexual behaviors.

There are six things that the LORD hates,
   seven that are an abomination to him:
haughty eyes, a lying tongue,
   and hands that shed innocent blood,
a heart that devises wicked plans,
   feet that make haste to run to evil,
a false witness who breathes out lies,
   and one who sows discord among brothers
(Proverbs 6:16-19).

If I believe homosexuality is a sin because the Bible declares it, does that mean I hate those who practice homosexuality? Does it mean I have no love for the gay community and homosexuals? Of course not. This conclusion may be the corner a spirit of tolerance attempts to paint me into, but it can't mean that. If calling a behavior sin rules out love toward the sinner, we're all caught in a logical, theological, and moral impasse. On the one hand, I could never love anyone because everyone is a sinner (Romans 3:23). On the other hand, I could never call any behavior sinful because that would be tantamount to hatred. More importantly, no one would be saved from sin because God could not love sinners.

So can I call a behavior sin and still love the sinner? Of course I can. I can declare drunkenness a sin and still love the drunk. I can and should treat the drunk with the compassion his human dignity requires. He is created by God. Furthermore, I am no more or less worthy than the drunk. Lest I seem to be picking on an easy target of socially unacceptable behavior…I can declare embezzlement by a white-collar businessman sin and still love the businessman. The point is, there is no contradiction between grace and truth.

The truth is indiscriminate in its assessment of the condition of mankind. Every last one of us is sinful and deserving of judgment. This includes homosexuals and heterosexuals alike. At the same time (here's the good news), the grace of God is just as indiscriminate. The homosexual is not excluded from the grace of God. What we have to keep in mind is obvious—believing that homosexuality is a sin does not also mean that being heterosexual gets you to heaven.

Finding Balance in the Cross of Christ

Balance is sustainable only in sight of the glorious truth of the gospel. Think about it. What is our message? It's the announcement of good news. God's Son has suffered the penalty of *sin* and accomplished what we were unable to accomplish. This earth is broken. We are all *sinners*. But Christ lived and died and was raised for us. When we preach the gospel of Jesus Christ, we demonstrate the balance of grace and judgment. God's hatred of *sin* is so holy and unrelenting that He punishes the sinner in eternal judgment. But at the same time, His love of *sinners* is so holy and unrelenting that He poured out His eternal wrath on His Son. Those sinners (such as I) who turn to the work of Christ by faith are forgiven and counted as righteous. The central message of Christianity (the gospel) is the ultimate harmony of grace and truth. It allows me to confront a behavior and love a person. The cross perpetually declares this reality. For on it we find God's righteous judgment of sin and His love for the sinner mingled together in infinite wisdom.

Point is, Christians need not retreat from the biblical perspective regarding homosexuality in order to love those who participate in the lifestyle (or to be seen as loving). But also, we need not shrink from showing compassion and grace to the gay community in order to sustain a biblical perspective. If the call of Christ conflicts with my politics, then my politics must change. There is no real biblical conflict here. Obviously, we may be rejected for holding an unpopular perspective, but that comes with the territory. As it is, we are called to serve and love all men, even those who most fervently oppose us.

I've found that when we are graciously honest and fervently (and consistently) compassionate, a helpful dialogue can take place. One in which both sides of the debate are informed by the other perspective. But if I'm imbalanced on either side, no such honesty is possible. If there is only compassion without truth, I'm merely hiding the biblical reality for a false peace. This is hypocrisy. If there is only truth without love, I'm misrepresenting the grace of God found in the gospel. This too is hypocritical.

Eventually, Christians must get around to what God says about sin. Even ours. The Bible is our authority—not politics or political correctness. Our goal is not to make Christianity appear acceptable to the masses. If this is our goal, we have lost already. The demands of Christ are ridiculous by design. We must answer the culture honestly. But in so doing we cannot co-opt conservative politics or family values and call it the gospel. They are not the same. If the gospel does not lead the way, we'll be pushed to one extreme or the other. The challenge is to stand between sin on one hand and grace on the other, aiming at the gospel in the middle.

I saw this very struggle take place with a notable evangelical who was invited to appear at a question and answer session led by a homosexual advocate. The event was organized to erase the prevalent stereotype of evangelical hatemongering among the secular community. Right out of the gate, the evangelical pastor was asked, "Is it a sin? Are homosexuals going to hell?"

The pastor's answer was vague at best. "The Bible has reservations… The Bible would say homosexuality is not God's original design for sexuality." No doubt it was a gracious attempt to arrive at a difficult truth through a more acceptable route. It was an obvious attempt to avoid the culture's knee-jerk response to Christianity. But the preacher appeared to lack conviction. Of course conservative Christians think homosexuality is a sin. That's what the Bible says.

Unsatisfied with an elusive answer, the moderator narrowed the question. "Is committing homosexual acts sin?" That's pretty direct. To which the pastor had no option but to answer yes. Eventually, you have to get around to the truth to retain it.

I Was Also Born This Way

Some people in the gay community (if not all) would argue that homosexuality presents a unique situation. I would agree. It is a complex issue. Some suggest we can't simply call it sin because in calling homosexuals to repentance you are asking them to abandon a lifestyle they did not choose. As the lyric of a popular song suggests, they were "born this way." How can they deny who they are? How can we call them to repent of their nature? Honestly, it's a great question.

This may sound strange (or heretical) to some, but I have no problem acknowledging that individuals may be born with a strong propensity for homosexuality. In the very same way, I have no problem acknowledging that certain people are born with a strong tendency toward heterosexual perversion. After all, every human being has inherited sinful DNA from Adam. We are all born with a corrupt nature that manifests itself in all sorts of idolatry.

> Therefore, just as sin came into the world through one man, and death through sin, and so death spread to all men because all sinned—for sin indeed was in the world before the law was given, but sin is not counted where there is no law. Yet death reigned from Adam to Moses, even over those whose sinning was not like the transgression of Adam, who was a type of the one who was to come (Romans 5:12-14).

In a sense, we are all "born this way." Of course, this is not to suggest that God is to blame for our condition. Paul made this clear as well: "All sinned." Is it any surprise, therefore, that homosexuality may be a part of our struggle as human beings? Similarly, is it any wonder people are born with a propensity for anger—a hatred of homosexuals for instance? Both are wrong in the eyes of God.

Ultimately, when the gospel is proclaimed, everyone is called to repent of who they are and how they live. Our nature is the problem. Our problem is not a moral one; otherwise, we could get better. It is a natural one. We are sick.

> As Jesus reclined at table in the house, behold, many tax collectors and sinners came and were reclining with Jesus and his disciples. And when the Pharisees saw this, they said to his disciples, "Why does your teacher eat with tax collectors and sinners?" But when he heard it, he said,

"Those who are well have no need of a physician, but those who are sick. Go and learn what this means, 'I desire mercy, and not sacrifice.' For I came not to call the righteous, but sinners" (Matthew 9:10-13).

This means that people's behavior is not the primary issue concerning their relationship to God. Behavior is the symptom of the real problem. The real issue is systemic. Homosexuality is not why homosexuals go to hell. In the same way, adultery is not why adulterers go to hell. Murder is not why murderers go to hell. Morality is not why moralists go to hell. Sinners (that includes all of humanity) go to hell because they are sinners. Sin may manifest itself in various behaviors. The point is, the gospel inconveniences everyone because everyone is in need of transformation. Drug addicts may be born with an addictive personality, but this does not excuse the destructiveness and idolatry of their addiction.

Heterosexuals need to repent just as much as homosexuals do. If we say they don't, then we are not preaching Christ correctly. Again, the gospel is nondiscriminatory in its declaration. All men are sinners. All men must believe in Christ's work to be saved. No exceptions. Moralists trusting their morality for salvation must repent of their "good" ways. Immoral folks ignoring their immorality must repent of their "bad" ways.

Shepherding the Marginal and Marginalized

I taught a seminar for our young adults and college students near a college campus titled "The Church and Homosexuality." We have a large and burgeoning population of college students and young adults at Community Bible Church. The aim of the lecture was to give this younger population a biblical frame of reference for the issue. Since they are on the college campuses and near the cultural centers, they are more inclined to encounter homosexuality. For certain, their generation is far more exposed than mine was at their age.

The takeaways were numerous.

• Knowing the biblical truth about homosexuality is not a license for hostility.

- We are called to love the gay community with the love of Christ.
- There is a sense in which homosexuality cannot be viewed with any more disdain than any other sin.
- At the same time, having a heart of compassion does not allow us to shy away from the difference in our perspective.

After deconstructing some long-held convictions, we took some questions and then fellowshipped around coffee. I was surprised by the number of people who thanked me for dealing with the subject. It was the first time many of those in attendance had heard any teaching on the issue.

But I was even more surprised by those who found the courage to open up to me about their own personal struggles in this area. In a sense, they were outing themselves. Some were practicing homosexuals who had heard about the lecture and joined out of curiosity. They adamantly disagreed with me on the core conviction, but they were stunned by a conservative Bible-believing pastor calling the church to serve the gay community. The dialogue with this group was healthy and informative. Others who struggled with the tendency and viewed it as sin found a compassionate ear.

Some of these ended up joining our fellowship. They are with us to this day. Being loved and loving others in the freedom of the grace of the gospel. They are part of the church, that strange and eclectic group of sinners saved by grace. We're an odd group indeed. But our variegated composition is part of our power. What else could draw such divergent backgrounds and people together?

Essentially, we've treated these members of our fellowship no differently than we treat any other sinner saved by grace—with love, truth, and accountability. We have walked with them through their various struggles in the same manner we do all our members. To assume no struggle exists in their lives after conversion is naive. This is how many ministries approach it, but we would not assume this with any other person or background. If an individual was saved out of a life of drugs, the addiction is likely to remain an issue and a primary temptation. This is reasonable to assume. And it is no different for those who have been saved out of a homosexual background. In fact, their struggle may be more intense, given the complexity of their former lifestyle. Coming alongside these brothers and sisters takes compassion and grace. The aim is not to engage in a sanctified "reparative therapy," but to point them to the transformative power found in God's Son.

I have great hope for love and victory. Somewhere Jim is always sitting across from me.

INSIGHTS FROM THE PAST

The reason Paul focuses on homosexuality in these verses [Romans 1:24-28] is because it is the most vivid dramatization in life of the profoundest connection between the disordering of heart-worship and the disordering of our sexual lives. I'll try to say it simply, though it is weighty beyond words.

We learn from Paul in Ephesians 5:31-32 that, from the beginning, manhood and womanhood existed to represent or dramatize God's relation to his people and then Christ's relation to his bride, the church. In this drama, the man represents God or Christ and is to love his wife as Christ loved the church. The woman represents God's people or the church. And sexual union in the covenant of marriage represents pure, undefiled, intense heart-worship. That is, God means for the beauty of worship to be dramatized in the right ordering of our sexual lives.

But instead, we have exchanged the glory of God for images, especially of ourselves. The beauty of heart-worship has been destroyed. Therefore, in judgment, God decrees that this disordering of our relation to him be dramatized in the disordering of our sexual relations with each other. And since the right ordering of our relationship to God in heart-worship was dramatized by heterosexual union in the covenant of marriage, the disordering of our relationship to God is dramatized by the breakdown of that heterosexual union.

Homosexuality is the most vivid form of that breakdown. God and man in covenant worship are represented by male and female in covenant sexual union. Therefore, when man turns from God to images of himself, God hands us over to what we have chosen and dramatizes it by male and female turning to images of themselves for sexual union, namely their own sex. Homosexuality is the judgment of God dramatizing the exchange of the glory of God for images of ourselves.

John Piper, "The Other Dark Exchange: Homosexuality, Part 1,"
Desiring God, October 11, 1998

NOTES

Chapter 1—Grace: The Outrageous Implications of the Most Delightful Truth Known to Man

1. Clark H. Pinnock, "The Destruction of the Finally Impenitent," *CTR* 4 (1990): 246-7.

Chapter 2—Sin: The Hairy Wart on the Witch's Nose

1. *Macbeth* (IV, i, 14-15).

2. Homer, *The Odyssey*, translated by E.V. Rieu (New York: Penguins, 1964), i., 4.

3. Jeremiah Burroughs, *The Evil of Evils* (Morgan, PA: Soli Deo Gloria Publications, 1992), 66-67.

4. Original source unknown.

Chapter 5—Hell: Grim, But Not a Fairy Tale

1. I will use the word *hell* to refer to the place where deceased unbelievers are now and for where people will be in the future— i.e., "the lake of fire." Technically, there is a difference, despite common vernacular.

2. Walter A. Elwell, ed. *Baker Encyclopedia of the Bible*, vol. 1, 1988. s.v. "Hell" by Ralph E. Powell, 955).

3. William G.T. Shedd, *The Doctrine of Endless Punishment* (New York: Scribner's Sons, 1886), 12.

4. Bertrand Russell, *Why I Am Not a Christian* (New York: Touchstone Books, 1957), 17-18.

5. From Jonathan Edwards's famous sermon "Sinners in the Hands of an Angry God."

6. John Blanchard, *What Ever Happened to Hell?* (Darlington, England: Evangelical Press, 2003).

7. John Calvin, *Institutes of the Christian Religion*, book 1, chapter 2, page 2.

8. Jonathan Edwards, *The Works of Jonathan Edwards*, vol. 2 (Edinburgh: Banner of Truth, 1974), 87.

9. As quoted by Harry Buis, *The Doctrine of Eternal Punishment* (Grand Rapids: Baker, 1957), 83.

10. Edwards, *The Works of Jonathan Edwards*, 80.

11. Charles Haddon Spurgeon, *The New Park Street Pulpit*, vol. 1 (Grand Rapids: Baker Book House, 1990), 308.

12. Christopher Love, *Hell's Terrors* (London: T.M., 1653), 19.

13. Blanchard, *What Ever Happened to Hell?*

14. Thomas Watson, *The Mischief of Sin* (Morgan, PA: Soli Deo Gloria Publications, 1994), 92.

15. Commonly attributed to Jonathan Edwards.

16. Joseph Alleine, *An Alarm to the Unconverted* (Edinburgh: Banner of Truth Trust, 1964), 64.

Chapter 6—Demons: Spiritual Swashbuckling

1. One notable exception is the excellent, biblical examination of demons by Alex Konya, *Demons: A Biblically Based Perspective* (Schaumburg, IL: Regular Baptist Press, 1990), 112.

2. Neil Anderson, *Bondage Breaker* (Eugene, OR: Harvest House, 1990), 107.

3. Anderson, *Bondage Breaker,* 111.

4. Anderson, *Bondage Breaker,* 179.

5. Fred Dickason, *Demon Possession and the Christian* (Chicago: Moody, 1989), 224.

6. Alex Konya, *Demons* (Schaumburg, IL: Regular Baptist Press, 1990), 112.

7. C.S. Lewis, *The Screwtape Letters* (New York: Macmillan, 1982), 3.

Chapter 7—Providence, Concurrence, and the Miraculous: When God Hacks into Life

1. Thomas Watson, *Body of Divinity* (Edinburgh: Banner of Truth Trust, 1958), 125.

2. Watson, *Body of Divinity,* 75.

3. Watson, *Body of Divinity,* 71.

Chapter 8—Unconditional Election: Curing the Vertigo

1. The Synod of Dordrecht: *The Canons of Dort,* First Head: "Divine Election and Reprobation, Article 7. Available online at http://www.spurgeon.org/~phil/creeds/dort.htm.

2. Peter O'Brien, *The Letter to the Ephesians,* in *Pillar New Testament Commentary* (Grand Rapids: Eerdmans, 1999), 100.

3. Technically, *election* stresses who is chosen, and *predestination* highlights how the choice was accomplished.

4. John Calvin, *The Epistles of Paul the Apostle to the Galatians, Ephesians, Philippians and Colossians* (Grand Rapids: Eerdmans, 1965), 125.

5. A.W. Pink, *Studies in the Scriptures,* vol. 5 (Mulberry: Sovereign Grace, 2001), 154.

6. Charles Spurgeon, "A Wise Desire," Sermon 33, delivered on July 8, 1855 at New Park Street Chapel, Southwark. Available online at http://www.spurgeon.org/sermons/0033.htm.

7. John Calvin, *Institutes of the Christian Religion,* ed. by John T. McNeill, vol. 2 (Louisville: Westminster John Knox Press, 1960), 926.

8. John Calvin, *Commentary on the Book of Ephesians,* Public Domain.

Chapter 9—Discerning the Voice of God: I Hear Voices

1. Benjamin Breckinridge Warfield, *The Biblical Review,* vol. 2 (New York: the Biblical Seminary, 1917), 169-82.

2. Martin Luther, *The Smalcald Articles,* part 2, article 2, no. 15. Available online at http://bookof concord.org/smalcald.php.

3. John MacArthur Jr., "Charismatic Chaos," part 2, audio sermon GC 90-53. Available online at http://www.jcsm.org/StudyCenter/john_macarthur/CHAOS2.htm.

4. E.Y. Mullins, *Freedom and Authority in Religion* (Philadelphia: Griffith and Rowland, 1913), 350-52.

5. Cited in J.I. Packer, "Calvin the Theologian," in *John Calvin: A Collection of Essays* (Grand Rapids: Eerdmans, 1966), 162.

6. Cited in Mark Bubeck, *The Adversary* (Chicago: Moody Press, 1975), 13.

Chapter 10—Committing to Church Membership: Anuptaphobia and the Bride of Christ

1. Paul Alexander and Mark Dever, *The Deliberate Church* (Wheaton, IL: Crossway Books, 2005), 60.

2. Joshua Harris, *Stop Dating the Church* (Sisters, OR: Multnomah, 2004), 16-17.

Chapter 12—Church Discipline: Taking the Fangs Out of It

1. John Calvin, *Institutes of the Christian Religion*, book 4, chapter 12, page 1.

2. J. Carl Laney, *A Guide to Church Discipline* (Minneapolis: Bethany House, 1985), 21.

3. G.I. Williamson, *Westminster Confession of Faith: A Study Manual* (Phillipsburg: Presbyterian & Reformed, 1964), 237.

OTHER GOOD
HARVEST HOUSE
READING

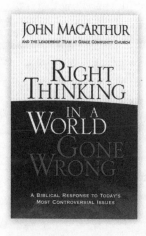

Right Thinking in a World Gone Wrong
*John MacArthur and the Leadership Team
At Grace Community Church*

One of the greatest challenges facing Christians today is the powerful influence of secular thinking. From all directions we're fed a constant barrage of persuasive—yet unbiblical—worldviews. This makes it difficult to know where to stand on today's most talked-about issues.

The leadership team at Grace Community Church, along with their pastor, John MacArthur, provide much-needed discernment and clarity in the midst of rampant confusion. Using the Bible as the foundation, you'll learn how to develop a Christian perspective on key issues—including...

- political activisim
- environmentalism
- the cult of celebrity
- entertainment and escapism
- homosexual marriage

- abortion, birth control, and surrogacy
- euthanasia and suicide
- disasters and epidemics
- immigration
- God and the problem of evil

Also includes a topical reference guide to Bible verses that address key concerns—a guide that will arm you with right thinking and biblical answers to challenging questions.

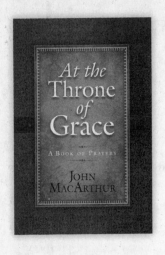

At the Throne of Grace
John MacArthur

Prayer is essential for every believer. Our heavenly Father lovingly compels us to come to Him with our praises, thanksgiving, and requests. He invites us to commune intimately with Him. And when we do, He is there. "Draw near to God," the apostle James wrote, "and He will draw near to you" (4:8).

This book is brimming with rich inspiration for your own prayer life. It's comprised of prayers spoken to the congregation at Grace Community Church—prayers that alerted the people that they are entering God's holy presence and standing humbly before His throne of grace. You'll discover how to pray more thoughtfully, more meaningfully, more worshipfully.